D0997201

THE STATE OF BRITISH ARCHITECTURE

THE STATE OF BRITISH
ARCHITECTURE

SUTHERLAND LYALL

THE ARCHITECTURAL PRESS · LONDON

For Heather, Peter and Mary

Picture Credits

Grateful acknowledgement is made to the following for permission to reproduce photographs. The name of the photographer, where known, appears in brackets. Architectural Association: 12; Architectural Press: 4, 5, 6 (bottom), 8, 9 (top and bottom), 13, 19, 21, 25 (top and bottom), 30, 31 (Richard Bryant), 33 (Sam Lambert), 35 (Henry Herzberg), 37 (top) (Dan Cruickshank), 37 (bottom), 46 (Tim Street Porter), 47, 59 (top) (D. McKenzie Chadwick), 62 (Martin Charles), 64 (Bill Toomey), 73, 76 (Martin Charles), 78, 80, 81, (Homer Sykes), 82 (Sam Lambert), 83 (top and bottom), 84 (Bill Toomey), 87 and 88 (Jo Reid), 89, 96 (bottom), 97 (top), 99 (John Donat), 108, 121 (top) (Tim Street-Porter), 121 (bottom) (Bill Toomey), 135 (Sam Lambert), 136 (Sam Lambert), 138 (top) (Bill Toomey), 139 (top and bottom) (D. Weld), 141 (Tim Street-Porter), 142 (top and bottom) (Deyan Sudjic), 149 (Deyan Sudjic); Arup Associates: 22; Brecht-Einzig Limited (all photographs by Richard Einzig): 32, 110, 116 (top and bottom), 127; Hedrich Blessing: 97 (bottom) (Bill Hedrich); *Building Design*: 6 (top), 11, 20 (bottom), 23 (John Goldblatt), 26, 27, 71 (John Mills), 77, 85 (top), 109, 113, 114, 115, 134, 143 (P. E. and M. E. Payne), 144, 145, 148; Martin Charles: 34, 129; Cement and Concrete Association: 59 (bottom), 147 (bottom); City Engineer, Newcastle-upon-Tyne: 138 (bottom) (G. Clark); Daily Post and Echo Limited: 43; John Donat (all photos by John Donat): 96 (top), 106, 117 (top), 120 (top), 124, 126; Farrell and Grimshaw: 118, 119; Keith Gibson: 128 (Keith Gibson); Greater London Council: 48, 90 (bottom); Sam Lambert: 137; Milton Keynes Development Corporation (all photos by John Donat): 24 (top and bottom), 75 (top and bottom), 105 (top and bottom), 117 (bottom); Martin Richardson: 10; Studio Vista: 38, 110.

First published in 1980 by The Architectural Press Limited, London
© Sutherland Lyall 1980

British Library Cataloguing in Publication Data
The state of British architecture.
1. Architecture, Modern—20th century—
Great Britain
I. Title
720′.941   NA968

ISBN 0-85139-081-1
ISBN 0-85139-082-X Pbk

Set in 11 on 13pt Apollo 645
Printed in Great Britain by
BAS Printers Limited, Over Wallop, Hampshire

Contents

Preface

This text is an attempt to assemble together one view of the story of British architecture over the last decade. That is the buildings of the last decade and the kind of thinking which lay behind them and which they, up to a point, made flesh. That way round rather than an examination of theory and design illustrated by buildings. This is not because I discount theory and design over buildings but because this is intended as a plain man's guide to what he can see of recent British architecture.

Anyone who has been at all involved in British architecture over the last decade will be offended in some way by inclusions and lacunae in this text. As the Smithsons said in a review of Reyner Banham's *New Brutalism*, 'Instant history has its hazards—the protagonists are still around; with their wounds half-healed, their minds fresh; and their archives in excellent order'. So that I make every advance apology possible to the archivists with sharp eyes and hard evidence and none particularly to the rest. It is unsafe for a journalist to have too many friends.

I must acknowledge the great help of almost all the architects mentioned in the book and more than a few unmentioned but in particular Christopher Woodward and Michael Foster. Colin Boyne commented very helpfully on the first draft. There is a continuing debt to my family who have put up with this in addition to the ordinary traumas of journalism, and to the *lieber Meister* Reyner Banham. Editor Lindsay Miller and I warred in genteel fashion over syntax, felicity of expression and style.

Introduction

Future historians of British architecture, in search of mainstream style and direction in the seventies, will have a hard time of it. For the seventies mark the official end of the Modern Movement—the apparently unified line of architectural ethic and aesthetic, philosophy and style which has sustained *avant garde* British architecture since the thirties and official and commercial British architecture since the late forties.

In its place is a conglomeration of attitudes to architecture which contemporary observers have viewed variously as simple disaster, as the new period of 'Post-Modernism', as, somewhat perversely, the culmination of the Modern Movement ideal and as what Martin Pawley has called a 'mixture of revivalism, *décor de la vie* and neighbourhood make-believe'.[1]*

Discounting the pejoratives, those interpretations of the architecture of the seventies are all more or less tolerable. What is not tolerable for many architects and critics is the absence of one single line of architectural development. On the one hand there is the neighbourhood make-believe of the 'Neovernacular' style now practised by most architects working for local authorities or local authority clients. On another is the high technology, industrial styling of Norman Foster, Rogers Associates and Farrell and Grimshaw, which is applied to everything from factories to housing. On yet another hand is the knowing and deliberate historical eclecticism of Campbell Zogolovitch Wilkinson Gough. And on yet another is the purist formalism of Christopher Woodward, the Grunt Group and early seventies' Milton Keynes architects. The preoccupations of the *avant garde* range from attempting to establish a basis for comment on architecture founded in Structuralism, through a simple revival of interest in the history of architecture, to the soft architectural designs of former Archigram hero of the sixties Peter Cook.

To the layman, the average architect and the traditional art historian all this sounds and looks like a mess, the last ramblings of the golden age

*Notes appear at the end of the book, on page 150.

of post-war British architecture. There is no unifying theme which observers can grasp and categorise, no dominant set of attitudes to which the ordinary architect in search of certitude can adhere. That pessimistic view is partly conditioned by the current introspective depression brought about by the drastic post-oil crisis reduction in the number of architectural commissions. But it is also conditioned by a false and simplistic view of the pattern of change and development in architecture—that which demands an identifiable, dominant line of mainstream architecture.

Selective histories of the Modern Movement

The notion of mainstream, that is of one inevitable and single kind of architecture which reflects the true spirit of a particular age, (the *Zeitgeist* theory), is a convenience devised by historians of design and architectural history. Borrowed from art history, it has been used relentlessly by historians of the architecture of the twentieth century. But as recent critics and historians, notably Reyner Banham, David Gebhard and Charles Jencks, have shown in various ways, the traditional single-line-of-development view leaves out large and important chunks of twentieth-century built architecture and architectural thinking and has distorted our view of the recent architectural past, and thus of the present also. It has done so because until now all the writers considered respectable in architecture schools and among architects have seen themselves as missionaries of the Modern Movement ethic and aesthetic: that is of the *ethic* of truth to materials and construction, of form as an absolute expression of the function a building fulfils, of architecture as a response to and expression of society (and mechanisation) in a rapid state of change; and the *aesthetic* of space enclosed by ordering planes, the absolute prohibition of applied decoration, separation of the elements of structure and geometric clarity of form—in practice the white wall, flat roof, pilotis and strip window of the International Style which characterised the early designs and buildings of many of the masters of the Modern Movement.

Nikolaus Pevsner, father of twentieth-century architectural history, left out Futurism and Antonio Gaudi in his seminal *Pioneers of the Modern Movement*[2] of 1936 because they did not fit into his construct of the Modern Movement. Gideon in his equally seminal *Space, Time and Architecture* argued: 'The world of history, like the world of nature, explains itself only to those who ask the right questions, raise the right problems. The historian must be intimately a part of his own period to know what questions concerning the past are significant to it . . . The historian detached from the life of his own time writes irrelevant history, deals with frozen facts'.[3] That standpoint justified a completely one-sided interpretation of modern architecture as the outcome of a line of structural and constructive innovations stretching back into the nineteenth century.

But David Gebhard, the Santa Barbara critic, has pointed out in his studies of all the rest of twentieth-century architecture the blindingly obvious fact (from a late seventies' point of view at least) that the written history of twentieth-century architecture was concerned exclusively with a tiny selection of the architectural output of the period. 'It is a mistake to see the history of the 20th century architecture which we have all been exposed to—from the *Pioneers* of Nikolaus Pevsner to Siegfried Gideon's *Space Time and Architecture*—as anything more than a handsomely designed historical construct . . . one of the most impressive sales pitches of our century, one which even Madison Avenue would find it difficult to match.'[4]

Reyner Banham, whose *Theory and Design in the First Machine Age* of 1961 effectively initiated the re-evaluation of the Modern Movement and filled in some of the more obvious gaps in Pevsner's pioneering work, was to point out in 1969 another important lacuna in traditional twentieth-century architectural history which, 'as it has been written up till the present time has seen no reason to apologise or explain away a division that makes no sense in terms of the way buildings are used and paid for by the human race, a division into structure, which is held to be valuable and discussable, and mechanical servicing, which has been almost entirely excluded from historical discussion to date'.[5]

These few preliminary revisions of the history of twentieth-century architecture have now been surrounded by an academic industry peopled by postgraduate students and academics, many of them centred on the Open University[6] who, following Banham and Gebhard, have begun to apply the techniques of art history to a period which hitherto has been thought too close in time for objective study, and some of whose major heroes were until 1969 still alive. Frank Lloyd Wright had gone long before in 1959 and le Corbusier in 1961, but Mies van der Rohe and Walter Gropius lingered on until the end of the sixties. Freed from their physical presence, historians and critics began to move in.

Much of this academic work has been a matter of revision and adjustment, and in the case of the study of mechanical services, expansion, but one recent right-wing group of Oxbridge historians, among them David Watkin, (author of *Morality in Architecture*, 1978[7]) has begun to throw the weight of highly selective academic research against the standpoints and postures of the heroes of the Modern Movement, in a campaign which is as one-sidedly antagonistic towards them as the histories of the post-war period have been overly sympathetic.[8]

Far better served by its press than any other profession in terms of quality and quantity of information—with three weeklies, five monthlies and a construction press numbering hundreds of journals—and by its professional and school lecturing circuits, the general tenor and often the detail of this academic work soon became known to and partly understood by most British architects, among whom it often

Eric Mendelsohn: Lukenwald factory, 1923

This and the following three designs belong to the early Modern Movement canon largely because of their contiguous dates. Subsequent historians have discerned a common Modern Movement architectural ethic which is supposed to unite them. In the case of all other buildings in the past the normal categories of *style* have been adequate and have continued to be used by these historian-proselytisers of the Modern Movement.

Opposite
Auguste Perret: Notre Dame le Raincy, 1923

amounted to no more than knowing that the 'death' of the Modern Movement was a respectable subject for conversation. A generalised feeling had percolated through that the early twentieth-century roots of their philosophy of design were withering, as the published postures of many of the masters were shown not to square with their practice.

What was less obvious was that the new research cumulatively revealed that the single-line, mainstream view of the pattern of architectural history was clearly inadequate. Not only had it produced a false overview of twentieth-century architecture but it had also contrived to lump all early twentieth-century *avant-garde* designs and buildings, many of them based on quite different aesthetic foundations, under the single Modern Movement banner. To the eye untrained by exposure to the Pevsner–Gideon construct, there seem to be obvious and fundamental differences between (quite at random) Mendelsohn's Lukenwald factory, Auguste Perret's Notre Dame le Raincy and Frank Lloyd Wright's Imperial Hotel, Tokyo—all of 1923—and Mies van der Rohe's glass skyscraper designs of two years before.

Traditional historians of the Modern Movement who accepted the standard art historical categories for the architecture of the past, which were based on recognisably distinct aesthetic foundations, suddenly shifted ground sideways into the realm of ethical classification when it came to the twentieth century. This was partly deliberate, because the Modern Movement sought to present itself as a *styleless* movement, a direct response to the programme of any building. But the inability of historians to explain satisfactorily the divergent appearance and apparently divergent aesthetic foundations of individual buildings in the Modern Movement went wilfully unnoticed by its proselytisers. Their need was to establish a numerical strength to support the credibility of the notion of a unified Modern Movement tradition, even

Frank Lloyd Wright: Imperial
Hotel, Tokyo, 1923

Mies van der Rohe: Skyscraper
design, 1922

when, by the early fifties, the three masters—Wright, Mies and Corb— had each developed mature and highly personal styles, behind which large sections of the architectural profession aligned themselves.

This sideways shift into ethics was an excellent, though not necessarily a conscious, tactic. It squared with the austere Calvinism of much of Modern Movement design and although it has apparently been noticed only recently, represented a reaffirmation, restated in the language of the twentieth century, of what architectural theorists have been saying in one way or another since the Roman writer Vitruvius: truth to materials and the methods of construction, form as an expression of function, architecture as an expression of society. What had changed was the meaning and emphasis which architects injected into these fundamental (and fairly unexceptional) principles and the aesthetic via which they made them flesh. This deliberate obfuscation of the difference between ethic and aesthetic *only* in the case of twentieth-century architectural commentary, coupled with the crude insistent of traditional architectural historians on graspable main-stream visual categories, has produced the illusion that the label Modern Movement is of the same order of visual description as say Gothic or Classical Revival, which it patently is not. In a sense the current public mourning by old guard architects at the death of the Modern Movement is simply a lament at the demise of an architectural historian's construct. If they had bothered to do as little as look backwards beyond the Modern Movement to even the nineteenth century they would have seen plainly that the history of architecture at any time has always been made up of a bewildering variety of approaches to putting buildings together and styling them. Architectural historians, in search of simplification for the sake of comprehensibility and employing a simplistic concentration on selected groups of buildings to fuel their personal view of what architecture *should* be about, have done us all a great disservice. As the remainder of this text should show, it is time now for both architects and their audiences to relax their search for the one true architecture: there are and always have been many paths to Nirvana.

The young lions

Out of this scene of re-evaluation and re-examination emerged a flourishing *avant garde*: in a state of critical confusion, individualism came to the fore. Issues of visual design and creativity once again became central following the days of brown rice as Peter Cook, grand maître of the young lions' kitchen, described early seventies' dogged dabblings in 'objective' design process and supposedly energy-efficient, low-cost Alternative architecture. But there were a number of important differences. The old fifties' and sixties' arguments about architectural morality, functional fitness and 'good' design had receded in favour of discussions about symbolic content and meaning, styling and wit. There was also a change from concern about the social

James Gowan: Neo-Purist housing, East Hanningfield, 1978

purposes of architecture to an interest in exploring and developing its pleasures.

Part of the change and part of the recovery of confidence by the *avant garde* had to do with the growing realisation, fathered by politically orientated young architects, that what architecture looked like or how it was designed was probably less important in achieving a level of satisfaction among its users than a building's management or maintenance or, in the case of housing, less important than the activity of tenants' associations and the policies of the government—by now the largest patron of architecture in the country. The expanding art of sociology produced studies which supported these somewhat negative conclusions.

If all this were true, ran the tenor of the never clearly articulated argument, then it was time to stop imagining that architects could somehow change the world. Planning committees and their officers, fire and building regulations, government cost yardsticks, mean maximum space standards, housing allocation officers and quantity surveyors—all these were beyond the sphere and control of the architect and yet were irremovably in his way. What architects were supposed to be good at doing was designing and thinking about architecture. It was time to start doing the things which architects could, in the real world, do well.

It needs to be said that this was easier for the theorist than the practitioner. Piers Gough put the *avant garde* architect's new position with a degree of bitter aptness in 1977: 'It makes me resentful and angry that I should be working in an era when the expectation level of the client, planners and the public is so low that one's most watered down schemes seem freaky . . . we have thrown away any consideration of seductiveness in style. Can't we drop this essentially moral miserableness that grips architecture and start to produce buildings that people might actually like—even sometimes, something that could be described as beautiful?'[9]

A representative enough attitude of the new *avant garde*, it was not to the taste of the old morality, personified by Martin Pawley, socially committed author of some of the best books of the decade on British

8

James Stirling: Olivetti training centre, Haslemere, 1970

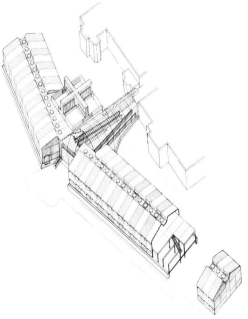

housing: 'The so called "post-modernists" . . . confess by their very "Pluralism" that no ideology, no vestige of social purpose, no unifying idea of the world animates their work . . . What is absolutely certain is that [there] . . . is no basis upon which the massively enlarged

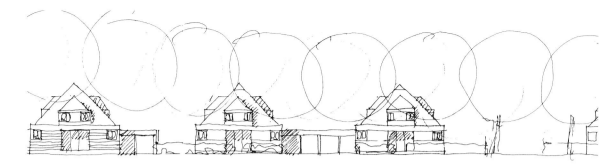

Martin Richardson: Project for developer housing in north Bucks, 1977

architectural profession of today can confront the problems of tomorrow'.[10]

Pawley in 1977 had at least got the point made by Jencks in his book of the same year *The Language of Post-Modern Architecture*,[11] i.e., that the new direction was towards new ideologies of design rather than of social purposefulness and that the *avant garde* did not mind very much if they were not all on the same path.

It was not as if many of the *avant garde* got to build very much in the post-oil-crisis years of austerity anyway. It was mainly the neo-Purist camp centred on the Grunt Group, based in the development corporation at Milton Keynes, who were able to transform revisions of Modern Movement styling into built architecture. In their case it was partly because of their concurrence with the orthogonal aesthetic preferences of chief architect Derek Walker, who was prepared to give free reign to his young designing lions. James Gowan's neo-Purist housing at East Hanningfield, based on Neoclassic and Renaissance forms, came into being largely because of the guardian angel rôle played by local officials. On the other hand designs for thirties-style developer vernacular (with built-in jokes) by Martin Richardson were either rejected out of hand or were given reality in nearby Milton Keynes sites in the form of Neovernacular and Neo-council-house public housing, with occasional unexpected high architectural spaces in discreet places inside at the rear. Only one of James Stirling's British designs of the seventies was built—the grp and glass Haslemere training centre for Olivetti—leaving a group of sensational glass plus neoclassic bricolage proposals on the drawing board. The winning scheme for a new town hall for Northampton, in the form of a vast glass pyramid by members of the Grunt Group, was in the end rejected by local councillors.

Straightforward rejection and the watering down of original conceptions is the standard lot of the *avant garde* in any period, and in the years of economic depression since 1973 there has been much time available for writing, talking, teaching and designing drawing-board architecture. The British *avant garde* is centred in London—almost exclusively in and around the Architectural Association school of architecture, with colonies in such London schools as Kingston Polytechnic, the Polytechnic of Central London, the Royal College of Art

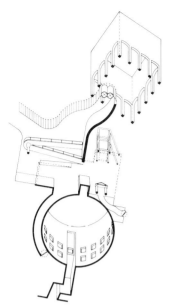

James Stirling: Three designs.
With the exception of
Haslemere (and the sixties'
designed housing at Runcorn
New Town, Cheshire), Stirling
has received no commissions
from British patrons. Outside
this country he is viewed, to
use Philip Johnson's words, as
the greatest architect in the
world.

Opposite
Detail from car park wall,
extension to Staatsgalerie,
Stuttgart, 1977. Ironic reference
to the ruins of classicism

Above left
Design for Museum of
Northrhine Westphalia,
Dusseldorf, 1975. Model and
axonometric of visitors' route
from below

Above right
Design for a political and
administrative centre for
Tuscany, 1978

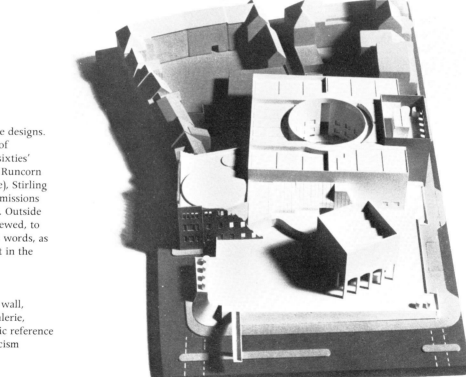

and the Bartlett. That has tended to be the case throughout the sixties and
seventies and although it is deprecated by non-AA based young
architects it is one of the facts of metropolitan-centred British culture. It
is a self-perpetuating tendency, for a teaching post at the AA has come to
stand as promotion to officer class from the other ranks of tyro
architectural innovators and revisionists.

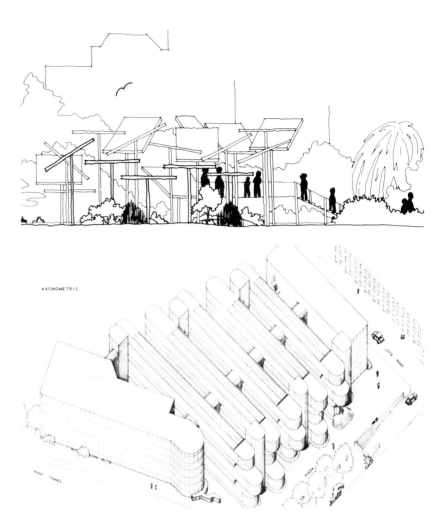

Associated with the AA was Art Net, run by former Archigram member and AA teacher Peter Cook. Funded for five years in the early seventies by art patron Alistair McAlpine, it is now a smallish art gallery in a basement near the AA, but in its heyday Art Net's ex-warehouse gallery was the venue for major exhibitions and discussions around the theme of architecture, its high point being a rally in 1976 of a worldwide selection of architectural designers and theorists.

A kind of homing instinct, coupled until recently with cheap rents, has clustered a surprisingly large number of young, ex-AA practices in Covent Garden, five minutes' walk away. Apart from the student audience and this built-in audience of local architects, who attend lectures by visiting foreign designers (giving the school its international cachet), the Association's most important public prop is *Architectural Design*; the monthly architectural journal which until the advent of the more or less AA-based *International Architect* acted somewhat uncritically as a mouthpiece for the AA-based *avant garde*.

A great deal of *avant garde* design is a matter of personal visual preference: Edward Jones' reworking of Modern Movement internal

Peter Cook: *Arcadia*, 1976; disintegrating town hall and shopping centre left, troglodyte suburb right

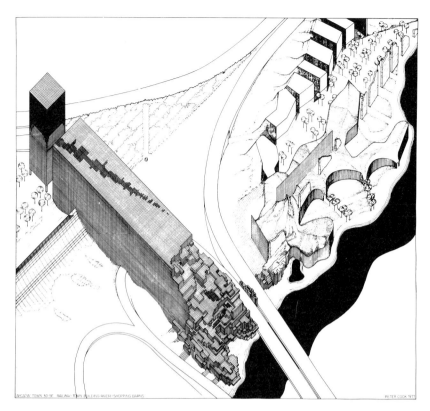

Peter Wilson: TWA pumping station and water house, Ministry of Drains and Humours, 1977

Ron Herron: Sets, 1977

spaces and external forms, Peter Cook's ambiguous arcadian visions of
bourgeois society, Ron Herron's sets for the ordinary and famous and
Peter Wilson's mysterious and surreal evocations of a sinister other-
world. At the same time the neo-Purists have developed visual games
based on Renaissance and Neoclassic forms and proportions restated in
unfamiliar contexts and others like Bernard Tschumi have moved to
straddle the traditional line dividing fine art and architectural
draftsmanship. On the other hand Leon Krier has developed an
architectural argument to do with architectural typology, based on a
Marxist critique of society.

   If there is any major theme among the *avant garde* it is probably that
of ambiguity and the deliberate juxtaposition of half-familiar images
from the architectural past in a way which deliberately flouts both
conventional architectural wisdom to do with consistency of styling
and public aesthetic conventions about architecture fitting in and
relating visually to the existing urban fabric. Although much *avant
garde* design is simply idiosyncratic, a significantly large number of the
avant garde employ ambiguity and stylistic incongruity in their search
for an architecture which can be interpreted in a variety of ways; an
architecture whose associative content is more important than either its
social purpose or its practical functioning.

   For a time in the seventies it was thought that this question of
interpretation—of providing a framework for architectural understanding and criticism—could be answered by the use of semiotics, the

14

Cross, Dixon, Gold, Jones:
additions to top floor of
warehouse in Covent Garden,
1977

theory of signs. Borrowed from contemporary European philosophy semiotics was pioneered in Britain by George Baird (author with Charles Jencks in 1969 of *Meaning in Architecture*[12]) and developed under the guidance of, among others, David Dunster and Geoffrey Broadbent. Based ultimately on the teaching of the late nineteenth-century scholar Ferdinand Sassure, semiotics (also known as semiology) attempted to order the pattern and nature of language. By examining basic distinctions and relationships with language according to a set of categories it was possible to come to some conclusions about meaning. Argument existed in some British circles about whether architecture was sufficiently equivalent to language for it to be susceptible to such analysis. But for the sake of what promised to be a serious and interesting academic task, the protagonists of semiotics merely affirmed that it was. With this stout conviction behind them they delivered a number of papers and lectures on the architecture school circuit.

Riddled with jargon which the critic and his auditors had to carefully learn by rote, architectural semiotics never seriously attempted to answer the question of whether it could be so readily transposed from language to architecture and what its useful function might be for all but students of the system. In retrospect its charts and mapping have the appearance of late sixties' attempts, notably by Christopher Alexander,[13] at arriving at a rational methodology of design—in the case of semiotics a rational mode of plotting, understanding and subsequently bringing about meaning in design. Missionaries of the new-found system pronounced in the press with some diffidence and suggested that further study and application were needed before the millenium of criticism came about or indeed, to quote Broadbent, before an understanding of how buildings actually 'carried' their meaning could be achieved.[14]

The useful outcome of this fascinatingly elaborate sidetrack was to direct the attention of critics (and to some extent designers) towards the possibilities of a multivalent architecture—away from the simplistic form-follows-function line of the Modern Movement towards a design

15

which could be 'read' at several levels or in different ways—an architecture which was rich and complicated in its symbolism and associations rather than the expression of a single-minded architectural ideology.

Much of the groundwork for this had already been laid by Robert Venturi's *Complexity and Contradiction in Architecture*.[15] First published in the USA in 1962, it was not widely read in Britain until around 1968 when David Gebhard used it as a basic text for a number of visiting lectures in London architecture schools. Subsequently the most influential architectural book of the seventies, it belongs to that long-standing tradition of historical writing in which a discussion of the past is used to put over a message pertinent to the present. Venturi's main historical discussion centred around Mannerist, Baroque and Rococo architecture, the architectures of deliberate complexity and high symbolic and literary content. 'I am for richness of meaning rather than clarity of meaning; for the implicit function as well as the explicit function. I prefer "both-and" to "either-or", black and white and sometimes gray, to black and white. A valid architecture evokes many levels of meaning and combinations of focus: its space and its elements become readable and workable in several ways at once.' And in a direct reference to the orthogonal simplifications of Mies van der Rohe and the Modern Movement he wrote: 'an architecture of complexity and contradiction . . . must embody the difficult unity of inclusion rather than the easy unit of exclusion. More is no less'.

That view squared with the dawning recognition that the Modern Movement reduction of the problems of a building to diagrammatic, 'rational' form, in which a selection of them could be solved, was an impoverished approach to design. Venturi celebrated practically everything that the Modern Movement ethic eschewed: ambiguity, multi-functional elements, the freedom to select and re-use motifs and forms from the whole heritage of architecture and the freedom to think of buildings not only as three-dimensional forms and spaces but as two-dimensional ensembles with fronts and backs, separate insides and outsides.

Although it was only in the USA that the architectural implications of the Venturi message were worked out and developed on any scale, the book provided a basic background for the *avant garde*'s movement away from architecture as social response to architecture as either art or architect's architecture, in which the juxtaposition of forms and details could be 'read' only by somebody reasonably well-versed in the history of architecture and its theory.

But to trace the influences on the built architecture of the seventies we must go back to the *avant garde* of a decade before.

Part One

LEGACIES

Architecture as structure

The British *avant garde* abandoned the Modern Movement as long ago as the late fifties. By the sixties they were celebrating the new pleasures of high and low technology, pop imagery, sensational structural design, the virtues of the temporary, *ad hoc* and deliberately incongruous, all carried out with a zest which mirrored the decade's heady feeling of an imminent Millenium. But it was sobered at its end by a worldwide student shift away from the visual pleasures of design, an over-preoccupation with which was held responsible for the alienating characteristics of public housing and official architecture. Reaction took the form of a dogged search for means of objectivising the processes of design and of an interest in design as a determinant of social behaviour. Thus only those parts of the sixties *avant garde* baggage which had an apparently 'objective' or small intuitive design content slipped through the Calvinist net into the early seventies. Most of these were based on new approaches to structure and construction.

Air structures

Few years around 1970 passed without one or another architecture school negotiating with local fire and building officers about the construction of an inflatable structure. These were attractive to students because air structures of impressive size could be built with builders' polythene, air conditioning tape and surplus store air pumps. They could be built in a small range of reasonably original forms and were large enough to contain the then standard student multimedia event and street theatre performance. Outside the student realm and outside the realm of student minimal technology, inflatables began to be taken seriously, notable by environmental artists and playgroup leaders but also by the government, which as early as 1971 had published Cedric Price and Frank Newby's *Research Report on Air Structures*[16] and later established a code governing their construction and safety.

Already in 1970 Foster Associates had designed and built an air structure for the rapidly expanding Computer Technology Limited. The firm's expansion plans were held up by planning bureaucracy and

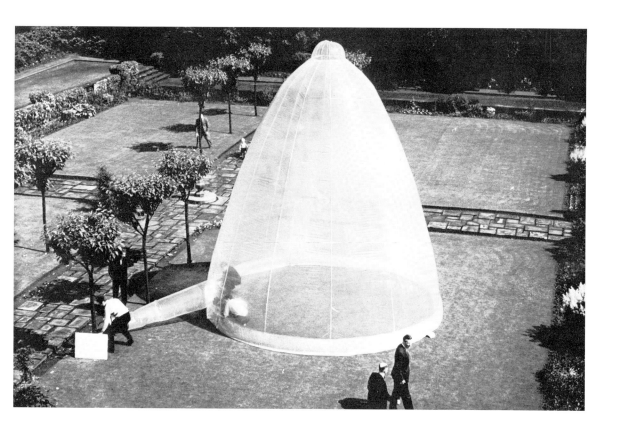

it had an urgent need for office space which was achieved temporarily
and with great elegance by a 600m long by 12m wide inflatable, in an
opaque nylon reinforced PVC fabric imported from Sweden. Inside, the
inflatable was equipped with standard office furniture and carpeting
and lit partly by natural light through the translucent skin and partly
by fluorescent lamps mounted on standards which also served as
supports for the skin should it either deflate or catch fire. The air
blowers doubled as warm air circulators.

With the energy crisis, the apparent lack of insulation and the
continual energy consumption needed to keep an inflatable up,
together with the probably petrochemical origin of the plastic skin,
combined to give inflatables a poor image and they fell from popularity
in the eyes of the young. But with the vogue for inflatables-for-
everything over, it became possible to work out uses, designs and
methods of construction which were appropriate. A good example is
former Archigram member Ron Herron's design for a portable theatre
for the travelling Bubble Theatre Company. The structure is a large
apsed barrel-vault shape made up from fat inflated arched ribs with
inflated 'pillow' panels zipped in between, forming the walls. The use
of double skins serves the dual function of providing a rigid structure
and insulating the interior from the elements outside.

No longer in the realms of fantasy (in Britain that is, for inflatables
had been used for decades in Scandinavia as temporary buildings) and

Adam King: Kinetic structure based on a development of the geodesic formula of small elements interacting to form a stable structure. Here the problem of cladding is solved by suspending a fabric skin inside.

Ron Herron and Pentagram: Bubble Theatre design, 1978

Graham Stevens: Desert Cloud, design for sun-powered air structure which at night lies flat on the ground and keeps soil humid; during the day it acts as a hot air ballon/carpet giving shade underneath

with their technology reasonably well understood, inflatables have lost much of their cult status even with late seventies' readjustment to high energy consumption. They are also outside the criteria used by financial institutions which traditionally back building, and their main future may well lie in the realm of airship design, which coincidentally featured in many of Archigram's sixties' images, and which at the very end of the seventies may begin to be financially respectable. The exception is perhaps Graham Stevens' design for artificial clouds for hot climates which deploy naturally heated air for their buoyancy—but these are unlikely ever to be seen in Britain's leaden skies.[17]

Lightweight structures

Geodesic and quasi-geodesic structures, first devised by Buckminster Fuller before the war, were a trademark of the alternative society of the sixties which carried through into the seventies. As with inflatables, they were attractive to architecture students because they could be built from small, cheap, lightweight members and because in some quarters they were seen to represent, in an almost mystical way, the ultimate development of a perfect irreducible geometric form, the tetrahedron. With properly designed joints they could also in theory be easily demounted. The difficulty with geodesics was not in conceptual design but in devising a waterproof cladding elegant enough to match the purity of the basic lattice form and in designing an inexpensive multi-directional joint to integrate both lattice and cladding.

Geodesics and inflatables, even in the small numbers in which they

21

Arup Associates: Bush Lane
House, Cannon Street, London,
1976. The water-filled steel tube
external lattice holds the
building up.

were built, figure as the major realisations of a number of sixties' and
seventies' preoccupations with lightweight and minimal structures.
Other ideas about at the time included foam plastic, grid shells, paper
construction and latterly, under the guidance of Florien Bagel at the
North East London Polytechnic, a kind of structure based on organic
stress analysis and the use of cheap components, usually timber. And
on the frontiers of engineering design Edmund Happold and his Buro
Happold, based in Bath where he is Professor of Building, have
continued to develop and design stressed membrane structures, many
of them in collaboration with the German designer Frei Otto and almost
all of them outside Britain.

The reluctance of British clients to accept anything other than the
rectilinear brick/concrete/glazing formula has meant that the
architecture-as-structure aesthetic has made little headway. The few
exceptions are really watered-down, built versions of the visions of the
sixties' *avant garde*.

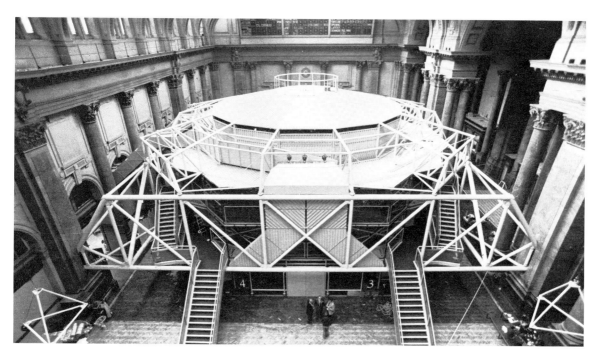

Levitt Bernstein Associates: Manchester Royal Exchange Theatre 1976—brightly coloured, deliberately incongruous module inserted into a listed Victorian interior.

Built architecture as structure

Arup Associates' Bush Lane House is a conventional enough glazed office block whose major vertical structural support is a diamond-patterned structural lattice *outside* the envelope of the building. Made from large hollow tubes of steel filled with water, the lattice supports the ends of the protruding floor beams. It is a design which is not only startling but partly a celebration of the frank use of structural steel. Although it forms an essential part of every large building's structure, the poor performance of steel in fires means that it is always buried in concrete. Here, by rethinking the whole issue of structural support and working out the minutiae of fire regulations, Arup Associates and their engineers Ove Arup and Partners have produced a building which reveals the true nature of the structural material and also meets fire regulations. At the same time the form and intricate patterning echo faintly and compactly some of the more exuberantly fantastic structural visions of the sixties.

Manchester's Royal Exchange Theatre travelled the sixties' structural *ad hoc* road rather further in the sense that it is an expressively structural object in the unexpected setting of the vaulted hall of a major nineteenth-century listed building. Supported on two great steel trusses spanning the base of the four buttresses to the hall's dome, the lattice framing and seemingly *ad hoc* steel decking (in fact located to allow an accoustic interaction between the theatre and the hall) contain seating for 700 people and a theatre-in-the-round stage. More than anything, this design by Levitt Bernstein Associates recalls sixties' images of highly serviced, high technology pods, dropped or plugged into the Piranesian ruins of a past age—ruins which it has been

Pierre Botschi, Milton Keynes architects: early development model (right) 1973, and built prototype mobile house (above) 1976. The structure was shipped in two halves and attached down the middle on site. Fittings and plumbing were already fixed in the factory.

too much bother to dismantle and too irrelevant to the vision of the future or present to take the slightest notice of.

Other seventies' built examples of architecture as structure have involved the use of sheet material, notably glass reinforced plastic, which in theory can be cast into shapes which are inherently self supporting. Such a rare building is the folded-paper-geometry of Pierre Botschi's grp sports pavilion at Bletchley and his prototype designs for grp houses for Milton Keynes. The built version of the latter is a single-curvature skin structure which retains of the original double curvature skin with zipped in windows only a curved eaves line and plug-in services redolent of sixties' preoccupations with total flexibility.

The problems of fire regulations and the cost of raw materials and moulds have in practice tended to relegate grp and other structural

J. Roscoe Milne Partnership:
Northampton Pigeon Fanciers'
club, 1977—blown up
industrial product design
aesthetic.

Fitch and Company: Vanessa
Redgrave Nursery School,
Hammersmith, 1972—
economical, cool use of grp in
combination with frankly
expressed trusses and other
structural and cladding
elements.

Opposite and right
Douglas Stevens and Partners:
Brunel Centre, Swindon, 1977

sheet metal materials to the role of cladding. An example is the J. Roscoe Milne Partnership's Northampton Pigeon Fanciers' Club, where the brightly coloured bands of grp are in fact panels on a concrete frame. Like the Botschi house, its aesthetic is redolent of blown-up industrial product design (such as coffee grinders and electric shavers), presenting a deliberate incongruity which also has its roots in the sixties. The coolest exception to this practical reality of the use of GRP has been Fitch and Company's nursery school at Hammersmith, where the major structural supports take the form of bright red grp apses, an inherently stable shape produced with the simplest kind of moulding technology. Where larger spans are involved, the designers have used standard open trusses which in most cases are simply seated into the apses.

Apart from the Pompidou Centre, discussed later, one of the most satisfactory seventies' architecture-as-structure buildings (although designed in the sixties) is Douglas Stevens and Partners' Brunel Centre at Swindon. Here low-level shopping malls are encircled and penetrated by vast glass half-barrel and barrel vaults, encased in open steel trusswork of heroic dimensions. From this group of shopping arcades rises a residential tower block (mainly for single people) clad in

27

curved cornered aluminium panelling and glazing, which owes not a little to the blown-up product design tradition (and in practice represents the high-quality, successful end of prefabrication). Here the official justification for what in the past was considered by large-scale developers as an unacceptable amount of exposed expressive structure is that it symbolises the achievements of the great nineteenth-century engineer Isambard Kingdom Brunel, after whom the centre is named.

The old guard

The seventies, like any period of architecture, has its old guard. Traditionally the kicking boy of the young and *avant garde*, there is a certain poignancy about the British seventies' old guard, for the ideological and stylistic battles in architecture are internecine and the sixties, parade ground of the old generals, has been so thoroughly discredited amongst architects and in the popular mind that the emergence of yet another of their productions is more a cause for polite embarrassment than righteous reaction. So long does it take to design and put up a large building in Britain that these old heroic productions, most of them designed in fact as well as spirit in the sixties, have come into view slowly but regularly through the present decade, dinosaur exemplars of the major Brutalist and megastructural thinking of a past age: Denys Lasdun's National Theatre and Institute of Education for London University, Neave Brown and Camden Council's Alexander Road, Basil Spence and Fitzroy Robinson's Queen Anne's Mansions, to name but a few. These buildings are not inherently bad, but the social, economic and cultural context in which they were designed has changed substantially over the decade. They are left, like twenty-stone, punch-drunk wrestlers, still lurching around the ring after the audience has gone out to eat fish and chips in the interval.

Brutalism

When Reyner Banham wrote the history of Brutalism in 1966[18] his final chapter was called 'Memoirs of a Survivor'; here he intimated that the British Brutalist contribution to the current worldwide architectural debate was over and that new things, such as James Stirling, were on the way. But for all that and although the style's high point is reputedly the Queen Elizabeth Hall of 1963, Brutalism in one watered-down version or another had by then become the *lingua franca* of the architectural establishment and had achieved acceptance as the way of designing public buildings. Brutalism's symbolic, or more accurately its expressive content was high. During the sixties, the end of a period of post-war austerity and the beginning of what was seen by many as a thrusting, aggressive, high-technology era, the craggy, lantern-jawed

Le Corbusier: Maison Jaoul,
Paris, 1953—archive for
subsequent Brutalist brick
detailing

and rugged honesty of Brutalism seems, in retrospect, to mirror the national self-image.

In his *New Brutalism* Banham reported Renato Peddio's list of the characteristics of the style.[19] They were a clear expression of structure, a high valuation of raw, untreated materials, clean virgin surfaces, heavy 'corrugated' volumes of prismatic simplicity, services exposed to view, zones of violent colour and picturesque groupings. In sixties' practice that meant off-the-form concrete, chunky forms and a set of details—board marked concrete, inverted 'L' windows, projecting nibs and external concrete balustraded staircases—straight from canonical buildings by Le Corbusier, the godfather of Brutalism. Corb's own buildings which were exemplary for Brutalism all dated from the period after the war when, as his antagonists put it, he had abandoned the pure hard forms of the International Style and 'gone soft' in favour of less orthogonal, more sculptural forms, based partly on an affection for peasant Mediterranean buildings and partly on a preoccupation with the patterning and casting of raw concrete: shown notably in his Maison Jaoul of 1953, in the pilgrimage chapel at Ronchamp and the roof-top structures of the Marseilles Unité d'Habitation.

There was a tendency for architects with Brutalist intentions to use or make visual references to one or more of Corb's details: Basil Spence's arched vaults on massive articulated brick piers and walls are blown-up versions of the domestic-scale vaulting of Maison Jaoul; Lasdun's staircase at the National Theatre (and those around the Queen Elizabeth Hall) are imitations of those to be found at Ronchamp and the Unité d'Habitation; and raw boardmarked concrete used by practically everybody with Brutalist pretentions in Britain. These are to be viewed not so much as plagiarisms but rather as reverential acknowledgements of Corb's inventive god-parenthood.

With official Brutalism went a tendency to monumental scale and with the passing of time since the uncompromisingly innovatory Queen Elizabeth Hall, a tendency towards more static grouping, a toning down of the exuberantly non-formal organisation of spaces and forms, and the use of materials other than concrete. The latter was not so much a watering down of the ruggedness of early Brutalism as an

Denys Lasdun: National Theatre, London, 1976—Corb-esque stairway middle right

John Madin Design Group:
Birmingham Central Library,
1974

Greater London Council:
Polytechnic of Central London,
building for the environment
school, 1971. This end and the
other give the impression of
being temporarily boarded-up,
waiting for subsequent
additions. There has however
never been the possibility of
that happening either at this
end or at the other. A gesture to
the idea of the possibility of
infinite extension.

appreciation of the fact that in Britain's climate concrete soon stained, grew lichen and occasionally developed stalagtites and suppurations. The last major echo of the Brutalist aesthetic was Denys Lasdun's National Theatre, completed in 1976. Apart from the absence of zones of violent colours and a disposition of forms which was centralising rather than picturesque, it conforms with the remainder of Banham's categories: boardmarked external and internal surfaces, theatrical structure (especially on the north and east corners where part of the structure is supported by raked concrete props), tall internal foyer areas interpenetrated by concrete stairways and walkways (connecting internal spaces and in some cases external terraces), and frank exposure of the internal workings of some of the theatres. For latter day observers it belongs to the expressionist end of Brutalism in the sense that it is rather more an expression of theatricality than of any particular architectural ethic; for the cynic its high degree of spatial and visual complexity echoes the high mechanical complexity of the stage machinery, which had prolonged teething problems.

The same spatially expressive and rugged game was played out in a number of seventies' old guard buildings. The John Madin Design Group's Birmingham City Library of 1973 deployed a startling inverted ziggurat on columns (based rather closely on Kalman McKinnel Knowles' Boston City Hall of 1964) with vast ceremonial escalators transporting readers up to the libraries arranged in hollow squares in the ziggurat above. Here expressionism for its own sake had taken over, for it is doubtful if readers or searchers after local history really require a metaphorical architectural fanfare every time they borrow a book. But the large-scale expressive game was irresistible. At the Marylebone Road site of the Polytechnic of Central London, GLC architects turned the problem of accommodating students and staff in

Neave Brown et al and London
Borough of Camden: Alexandra
Road housing, 1978

studios, offices and teaching rooms into a major piece of internal spatial and structural drama. Vertical circulation and service runs (in fact mostly stairways, lifts and lavatories) are denoted by a set of large concrete towers, between which is slung office, laboratory and studio accommodation; the towers also support an oversailing loft of studios. This difficult piece of structural engineering (and as it turned out difficult construction as well) was required to allow a vast two-storey space with balcony studios ranged on either side to run right through the upper floors of the building.

The Polytechnic building is also of interest because it managed to incorporate intimations of megastructure. The end walls of the main block along Marylebone Road were left panelled in metal decking, with the ends of beams and slabs exposed—rather as if the building had been sliced off and its ends temporarily boarded up; but as the building stretches the full distance of the site and cannot go further (unless it is built over the side road), these suggestions of infinite extension are no more than a gesture in the direction of megastructure.

Megastructure

One of the major recurring themes of discussion and drawing board design of the sixties, megastructures were, to paraphrase the going definition, enormous structures theoretically capable of infinite extension, composed of modular, repetitive units which fitted, visually if not in reality, into a structural framework. As Peter Hall derisively put it 'like everything at Montreal's Expo 67 rolled into one and built about a mile high'—or, more accurately, long. Not quite that long is the 250m curve of the Borough of Camden's Alexandra Road housing. Arranged in layers of terraces, it leans its almost blank back over a noisy railway line to form an acoustic shield for the rest of the tightly packed site, which contains housing, community and special buildings and an underground car park. The profiles of the projecting party walls of the curved housing 'wall' zig-zag diagonally up to the seventh floor, the stepped-back terraces giving all the south-facing flats good light even in winter and allowing private garden patios in front. The terraced section belongs to a family of sixties' designs: the central spine of Thamesmead, the 1974 Utopian Housing scheme behind Marble Arch and Patrick Hodgkinson's Brunswick Centre in Bloomsbury, as well as any number of designs published throughout the sixties; which probably also owe something to the Futurist sources of the Brunswick Centre. The Centre was planned to be extended northward, but houses in the way of what was already a small megastructure were refurbished instead. A few blocks away is another megastructural building, Denys Lasdun's Institute of Education. Probably the most monumental building in London, it stretches the entire length of Woburn Square along Woburn Way. It is composed of a long, horizontal, glazed block, jacked-up two storeys in

Patrick Hodgkinson: Brunswick Centre, Bloomsbury, 1968— compare with the Sant' Elia apartment block

Antonio Sant'Elia: Apartment
block, pre-1914

the air on concrete columns. Concrete block houses with triangular
roofs squat at regular intervals half under the glazed range. With the
overhanging tops of its tall concrete service towers, the ensemble looks
from certain views in the street like a set of misaligned jaws clamping
the horizontal block two stories up in the air. Insufficiently clear in its
metaphor, if such was ever intended, the building reads merely as an
example of large-scale, out-of-context expressiveness.

Of course not all large buildings are megastructures and the seventies
saw the completion of a number of buildings which were simply very
big. They include the latter stages of the Barbican centre (which had
been building since the late fifties) the National Exhibition Centre at

Denys Lasdun: Institute of
Education, Bloomsbury,
London, 1978

Building Design Partnership:
Halifax Building Society
headquarters, Halifax, 1975

Birmingham, Arundel Great Court, occupying an entire block on the
Strand, Eldon Square shopping centre in the middle of Newcastle and
the great Halifax building society headquarters in Halifax. Enormous
buildings or groups of buildings all, they mainly demonstrate their
designers' personal preoccupations. With the exception of the
enormous lozenge-shaped Halifax building, apparently two storeys of
curtain-walled offices mounted on four enormous legs (which
occasioned jokes about dinosaur-like creatures) they did little more

than impose their vast bulk on their surroundings.

Megastructures were more than just enormous buildings: they were intended to serve the complete range of activities of urban living and their scale was a function of the multiplicity of activities which took place within them. Thus the Brunswick Centre has housing, car parking, shopping and entertainment facilities, including a cinema. Alexandra Road contains housing and local community social facilities including a remand home and dwellings and a school for disabled people. The earlier, later sixties' proto-megastructures of the new towns such as Cumbernauld and Runcorn also incorporated most of the major functions of civic and residential life in vast rambling constructions which were intended to grow and accrete. This notion of the city as total architecture had its origins in a number of popular sources.

Apart from le Courbusier's Fort l'Empereur for Algiers of 1931, which is reckoned to be the unbuilt model for the megastructure idea. important notional megastructure sources were Sant'Elia's vast Futurist multifunctioning transport interchanges and housing designs of before 1914 (whose raked walls and buttresses were the source of the diagonal sections of British housing megastructures), the film sets for such movies as *The Shape of Things to Come* and *Metropolis*, and any amount of science fiction literature and cinema about large-scale closed communities in inimical landscapes. Evocative designs of the sixties included Hollein's half-buried aircraft-carrier city schemes of the mid-sixties, Yona Friedman's Spatial City of 1961, Habraken's Supports Structures, Rudolph's Lower Manhattan Expressway project of 1970 and Ron Herron's Walking City project of 1964, a totally mobile city which walked from one source of nourishment to another and recalls (co-incidentally) the series of science fiction stories by James Blish about cities which take off complete with self-contained environments from the exhausted Earth to carry on itinerant existences in the reaches of outer space.

Megastructures promised to provide the social integration which those Utopian schemes and stories depicted—and, not least important, brought the designer of this total architecture right into the centre of the social arena. Megastructure was prime territory for megalomania.

Apotheosis

Apotheosis or more accurately *envoi* of the whole megastructural and Brutalist discussion was Ivor de Wofle's *Civilia* of 1970 and a special issue of *The Architectural Review* of late 1973 on the same theme[20]—a vision of a brutalist megastructural new town to be located on a set of waste heaps near Coventry. It was illustrated by a series of photomontages taken from sixties' issues of the *Review* and masterminded by H. de Cronin Hastings, chairman of the Architectural Press and major publisher and champion of modern architecture since the thirties.

Hastings' usual pen name was Ivor de Wolfe and the transposition Wofle was lost on all but a few regular readers of his work whose suspicion was that the book might be a joke, a last two-fingered gesture

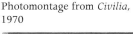

Photomontage from *Civilia,* 1970

to a confused profession on the eve of the retirement of this enigmatic *eminence grise* from architectural publishing. The suspicion deepened when the illustrations turned out to be juxtapositions of all the famous Brutalist buildings of the previous decade: part views of Thamesmead and the Brunswick Centre forming backgrounds to sections of Lillington Gardens and the Post Office Tower, buildings by Powell and Moya and Lionel Brett jostling cheek by jowl with pebbledashed and boarded local authority housing schemes—and in one case a building which on closer inspection turned out to incorporate part of a Brutalist building on its side dramatically cantilevered over a Thamesmeadesque lake.

Received cautiously by an architectural establishment which had not picked up any ambiguity and which was uncomfortable about the pastiche mode of illustration, it represented for the young the outdated megalomaniac fantasy world which their elders seemed determined to inhabit. Joke, ambiguity or not, Hastings' passionate editorial in the follow-up *Review* issue scythed through the received wisdoms of the time: design methodology, official planning and what he saw as the non-event of the new towns. 'More productive, perhaps, naive and simplistic though it seems, to stay with the vocabulary of art and try to reassert the designer's right to think graphically rather than abstractly or mathematically or pragmatically or politically: to side step the formulae of sociologists; to duck out from under the straight-jacket imposed by bureaucrats; to reassert the citizen's need for fun, wit, sociability, variety, drama in his architectural environment, not excluding his home and so bring the lyrical possibilities of an advanced technology into play. The alternative to dreaming things up is non-eventism.'

Despite the accompanying illustrations and a plea for very high density close-packed housing, these sentiments were remarkably prescient of the spirit of late seventies' architects, for whom individual talent and creativity was no longer something to be self-consciously abjured. But as far as the megastructural solution was concerned critics have argued that in avoiding the unsociable height of sixties' tower blocks megastructuralists have missed the point that sheer size may well be one of the important factors in creating social stress. Where the tower blocks could theoretically be surrounded by green landscaping, neither the Brunswick Centre nor Alexandra Road allow very much open space. The Brunswick Centre has none apart from the square across the road. Alexandra Road has a pitiful row of small rectangular landscape areas, each heavily loaded up with play equipment or mounds, a situation which the proposed hanging planting in the boxes across the front of each flat can hardly put right. By the mid-seventies megastructures were out of fashion anyway and only the eighties can properly tell whether gloomy prognostications about what happens to people living in monumental housing are true or not.

Disasters

Whatever the state of architectural design and thinking in the seventies, the decade has been one of disaster for practising architects. The disasters have been so numerous that it is unlikely that the British public will ever again entirely trust its public architects in the accepting and even encouraging way it did in the fifties and sixties. In those post-war reconstruction days architects, particularly housing architects, were seen (and certainly saw themselves) as a critical element in the creation of a bright and beautiful new Britain.

Important, and even crucial, architects certainly were in changing the face of post-war Britain. But too many of them grossly over-reached themselves in terms of technical understanding, in realising only shoddy imitations of revered architectural and planning theories and in mistakenly transforming a sincere personal commitment to the creation of a better physical environment into a belief that they were thereby fully fledged social engineers, prime instruments of significant and progressive social change.

The beginning of the end of the special post-war relationship between architects and the public was signalled by the collapse of Ronan Point in 1968. A prefabricated multi-storey housing block made of slabs of concrete walls and floors stacked together like a house of cards, much of it progressively collapsed when a gas explosion at a high level blew out an external wall. Five people died and 200 people were made homeless. A failure of the details of a construction system, Ronan Point quickly came to symbolise the failure of architects to deliver what they had promised—comfortable and well designed housing for all; it was the anticipation of their ability to do just that, and soon, that had limited the effect of conservative popular objection to the styling and scale of modernist post-war housing.

Tower blocks
The massive failure of public confidence in high-rise public housing was given credibility by the results of several social surveys on high-rise life. Newspaper and telelvision propaganda against its supposed ills soon made the results of any further 'objective' sociological surveys

hopelessly biased for a number of years. It must be said that one or two surveys carried out in early 1978 demonstrated the not entirely surprising fact that some tenants enjoyed living in high-rise blocks and that the provision of caretakers and an answerphone and other facilities allowing reasonable supervision of callers made high-rise living perfectly acceptable—especially when the teenagers and children of the late sixties had grown up and moved out.

But at the beginning of the seventies none of these things had happened, nor was the public's perception of high-rise living anything other than inimical to it. At that time architects were clearly seen to have failed in their self-appointed role of social engineer: they had conspired to design family dwellings physically divorced from the street life which had been a fundamental part of English urban working-class life for centuries.

At the heart of this failure was the attempt by architects to bring about upward class mobility, from tightly packed slums into a bright and beautiful middle-class technological world. It was done in a way which, however much based in genuine concern and sincerity, was ultimately patronising, authoritarian and insensitive. Given the methods of local authority housing allocation departments it was cold-bloodedly callous—for there was no effective choice for people on a housing list. The price of progress was effectively that people could move into tower blocks styled and designed on the basis of the architectural and planning ideology of the new age or rot in their slums, which were probably scheduled for demolition anyway.

Although high-rise living was a middle-class urban tradition in many parts of Europe—and in America for the wealthy—this was not the case in England. British tenants simply had no experience of tower blocks; nor had the architects and housing committees responsible for them—although they congratulated themselves that they were giving the inadequately housed worker population not only new housing but housing in a form associated internationally with middle- and upper-class life. Tenants moving from the old street life had to make fundamental changes in the way they lived (this was part of architects' and housing committees' patronisingly benevolent intentions); but because parsimonious local authorities conveniently forgot the necessary adjuncts of high-rise living abroad—*concièrges*, porters, high maintenance and repair services and high quality finishes and construction—changes in tenants' patterns of living were not in the direction of upward social mobility but merely changes to meet a more constrained physical existence. Families with children could no longer leave them to play in the street or in the back yard, maintaining a loose surveillance at close proximity. No longer was it possible to make the casual passing acquaintance of the street, since the only point of social contact in a tower block was the lift and entrance lobby, with four or five blank front doors (rather than a street full of windows and doors) indicating the existence of neighbouring families. When inadequately

Blow up: Oak and Eldon
Gardens, Birkenhead at the
instant of being blown up,
1979. These 1958 blocks for 900
people had become so
unacceptable to council tenants
that this extreme step had to be
taken.

serviced facilities broke down, particularly lifts, tenants were faced
with sometimes acute physical inconvenience simply because they
were obliged to live on the upper floors of the product of a
megalomaniac architectural and planning theory.

Vandalism, which was often the cause of breakdowns in services and
the obvious cause of visually appalling environments, was seen to be a
concomitant of tower blocks and the connection attracted much
attention in early seventies' denunciations of high rise. It has clearly
been a contributory cause in the recent abandonment of a number of
sixties' tower blocks—for example in the Wirral and Liverpool, where
in 1979 local authorities decided to demolish or blow up wrecked or
uninhabitable tower blocks scarcely fifteen years old.

Recent government studies, however, suggest that the size of the
adolescent child population in an estate, rather than simply tower-
block living, is the crucial element in vandalism. For example, low-rise
Corby New Town, much admired by such early low-rise propagandists
as Nicholas Taylor, has suffered appalling vandalism in much of its
two- and three-storey housing and some of its comfortable community
centres. If this equation between vandalism and the adolescent
population is correct, then vandalism in late sixties' and early
seventies' estates was almost inevitable, for families with three or more
children had high priority on housing waiting lists. In designing family
dwellings in tower blocks, architects were not only designing-in

misery but, inevitably, the recipe for auto-destruction. In normal circumstances architects could have excused themselves from much of the blame by pointing out that they were merely the instruments of housing committee policy and were dealing with a form of housing which was alien and unfamiliar to them. Although the latter was clearly the case, architects had got a severe case of the 'social engineers' and had too often and too confidently accepted a great deal more responsibility for tower blocks than was theirs. And thus they found themselves making overly dramatic public confessions of failure through the early and middle part of the seventies.

Almost worse than the public repudiation of tower blocks was the implicit rejection of the deeply cherished Modern Movement town planning theory, centred on Le Corbusier's *Ville Radieuse*, from which the theory of tower blocks sprang. It was an implicit rejection, for few people outside the circle of architects and planners were aware of the existence of the theory or the vision. A 'rational' response to the 'densely packed quarters and congested streets', ill-lit courts and lightwells of early twentieth-century European slums, Corb's vision was of enormous housing constructions sixty stories high, scattered around great parks of trees. From all the windows of these great constructions there would be uninterrupted views, 'starting from the fourteenth floor you would have absolute calm and the purest air'. Corb's tower blocks were designed to rest on three and four storey high pilotis, or legs, so that the landscape would visibly flow through and under the mass of the buildings. Ham-fisted British local authority architects could not resist the temptation to fill in this 'waste' space with functional things like additional floors of flats, dustbin stores, lift lobbies and the like. In Corb's vision the services and circulation infrastructure was all underground. In addition, tower blocks in the middle of British cities were set, not in rolling waves of foliage, but banal municipal lawns and vandal-proof stretches of concrete and tarmac. Nor was anything seriously provided in the way of services or social or community infrastructure. A gesture had been made in the direction suggested by the illustrations of the 'City of Towers' of 1920–3 and, as is the manner with copyists, this was as much as anybody could get around to doing.

With no more evidence than his personal conviction, Corb had assumed that the quality of life in his worker towers would be better than in the tightly packed streets of nineteenth-century slums. This simplistic belief was taken over by British architects and planning committees with great conviction but with as little evidence. Their main aim was to provide new, clean and decent, modern accommodation for the post-war British working classes, whose standard of physical life had not changed very much since the nineteenth century. And that was what Corb's vision offered. But by the beginning of the seventies the reality was not enough.

System build

Ronan Point was a prefabricated concrete system building whose joints and method of construction turned out to be inadequate. Its collapse gave technical credence to popular dislike of the machine-like appearance of mass-produced municipal system buildings. During the sixties local housing authorities had erected hundreds of estates in one or another of the 300 systems on the British market by the end of that decade. Prefabricated buildings were not particularly cheap but they were normally quick to build. Cheapness came with very long production runs and that never really occurred within the local authority system of tendering. But speed was what the housing crisis was seen to need. As the seventies have progressed it has become clear that too many of these prefabricated systems were put together too quickly. Many of them were discovered to leak water into the interiors, and in the case of system tower blocks at Portsmouth and Hillingdon it was discovered after taking down spalled concrete cladding panels that the basic structure of load-carrying walls and floors had become severely weakened. The cost to Portsmouth local authority of repairing two tower blocks was estimated at over £1·5 million, and Hillingdon had repair bills of between £6 million and £14 million. Nearly 50,000 units of this particular type of construction were built in the sixties.

Although in practice architects had very little understanding or experience of this novel form of building—often simply arranging layouts to meet government space standards and signing off certificates of completion—the *idea* of prefabrication and standardisation was close to the centre of Modern Movement thinking. Walter Gropius once said 'We are approaching a state of technical proficiency when it will become possible to rationalise buildings and mass-produce them in factories by resolving their structure into a number of component parts. Like boxes of toy bricks, they will be assembled in various formal compositions'; Le Corbusier and other Modern Movement architects

Greater London Council
architects' department:
Thamesmead spine block,
1967—prefabricated aesthetic
but built on site

had said the same thing with equal conviction since before the Great War.

In post-war England the CLASP (Consortium of Local Authority Schools Programme) lightweight steel frame and panel system, used widely for school buildings, seemed to realise the prefabrication dream. It not only worked in building terms but had the orthogonal aesthetic and structural 'honesty' of the Miesian end of the Modern Movement. So expressively modern was it that when CLASP turned out to be too expensive for one stage of Robert Matthew Johnson & Marshall's York University the architects put up conventionally constructed buildings which imitated one of the variants of CLASP's external forms: a strange inversion of the normal scheme of things in which traditional cladding is used to conceal a factory-made inner structure.

Something of this sort was also to occur at Thamesmead where the GLC set up an industrialised building factory which produced the components for much of the new housing in this overspill development on the Thames marshes, not far from Woolwich. The centrepiece, a long snaking string of housing, was to have been the first of the industrialised buildings, but political pressure to get work started immediately resulted in this spine group being put up in standard poured in situ concrete construction which imitated prefabricated construction.

46

The *beau ideal* system building was one produced entirely in the factory, shipped ready plumbed and serviced to its ultimate destination in a supports structure or green field site with an underground services network—and there plumbed in. It was an idea which was implicit in a great many megastructure designs of the sixties and was explored most notably by the Archigram group in its Plug In City of 1964. In 1967 that bubble was deflated somewhat when word got around about the incredibly high cost and the degree of compromise involved in building Moishe Safidie's Habitat at the Montreal Expo. An artificial hill town of individual concrete prebuilt flats which were stacked in their final casual array by crane, it suffered from the standard teething problems of pilot projects: not enough built, rather more work having to be done on site than was anticipated, greatly inflated costs in consequence and difficulties with linking up factory fixed plumbing. Habitat was not a conspicuous failure but its form, redolent for British observers of primitive hillside villages, was already slightly out of date for the *avant garde* and the plug-in aspect of Habitat were not much followed thereafter in Britain.

The promise of system building was never properly realised. Dwellings could be produced in a relatively short time once a system got going but they were expensive. There were too many systems competing for a limited market and those that got built tended to be one-off exercises. Without long production runs, tooling-up costs could only be offset by high initial unit prices. Even Thamesmead, probably the largest single prefabricated housing operation in Britain,

Moshe Safdie: Habitat, Montreal, 1967—artificial cliff of prebuilt and stacked dwelling units

47

Greater London Council architects' department: Farm Lane, Fulham, 1976. Units containing bathroom, kitchen and entrance were shipped from Holland, and stacked three high on site. Precast beams bridging between adjacent stacks formed the living room floors. The whole was then given a skin of brickwork and an entirely conventional appearance.

folded up and had its factory razed as soon as government cost yardstick criteria were applied to it.

That has been true of concrete systems. But in the late seventies prefabrication has been taken up more successfully by timber manufacturers. Formerly an expensive material, timber has, after the wild fluctuations in the price of building materials around 1973, become economic. Although prefabricated wall and floor panels are still relatively unusual, prefabricated timber roof trusses are the rule rather than the exception on late seventies' housing sites. Almost inevitably for the disaster-ridden seventies, doubts were raised in 1978 by engineers in the technical press about the structural performance of trusses which had been inadequately stored on site.

The problems of system building and prefabrication (the terms are almost interchangeable in common parlance) hinge on the size of basic units, transport, quality control and tolerances. The Gropius vision of factory-made homes staked together on site has to be tempered, in Britain, by the impossibility of transporting loads of more than a certain width. A Greater London Council experiment with this approach at Farm Lane, Fulham, ended up with half units containing bathroom, kitchen and entrance hall being shipped in (from Holland) and the remaining rooms constructed in traditional fashion on site in between the prebuilt units, using the prefabricated shells as structural supports.

The theory of total building prefabrication was one aspect of the Modern Movement preoccupation with machine made, mass-produced goods, and under this doctrine it was believed that the imprecisions of on-site workmanship would be obviated by putting together as much of a building as possible under precise factory conditions. What architects forgot, or more probably never investigated, was the high rejection rate of components in even low precision industrial mass-production processes. The occasional sub-standard plastic toy can be thrown out, but it is less easy to know what to do with expensive massive concrete panels which are below quality control standards. The reality became clearer when at Thamesmead and in other prefabricated system-built towers, precision factory-made units failed to match up to the high degree of accuracy demanded by the architectural drawings, and workmen adding the crucial final sealing and jointing carried out the work only to ordinary on-site standards.

Even when a high degree of precision casting could be achieved, as with glass reinforced plastic, there were problems with the technical processes involved. In 1976 the GLC had to spend nearly half a million pounds on replacing gasketted opening windows in the prefabricated grp panels on a number of tower blocks in London. Most of this cost was to do with replacing leaking semi-pivoting windows but because some of the neoprene gasketting had failed it was all replaced with metal clip-on framing.

The result is not that prefabricated systems have been rejected, but during the course of the seventies it has become clear—and will become clearer in the eighties—that the full implications of system building have not been thought through, either by engineers or architects or their promoters.

Materials and techniques

The fifties and sixties had been a time when new and potentially exciting materials and to an extent techniques came on to the building market. In the seventies a significant number of them began to fail.

Flat roofs, the trademark of the Modern Movement, were inherently difficult for the ordinary builder to construct to the required degree of accuracy—at least on the scale of domestic building. They leaked with such regularity that they became the standard butt of opponents of Modern Movement architecture, who were now given gratuitous practical evidence to support their personal visual preferences. By the mid-seventies some local authorities had developed the solution of constructing timber-framed tile or asbestos slate roofs straight on top of the flat roofs on fifties' and sixties' estates which were now proving so inadequate.

Condensation was a new problem. It was partly a consequence of local authority parsimony and inadequate public standards of insulation, but the profession was to bear the brunt of this failure to understand the problem of cold bridges and skimpy construction, exacerbated by tenants who now demanded a much higher level of warmth in their houses, only possible with central heating.

The behaviour of new materials under stress was not well understood either. A number of people died when fire gutted a new leisure centre on the Isle of Man which had been roofed with translucent acrylic. Locked firedoors were responsible for many of the deaths but no one thought of the effect of melting acrylic dripping from the roof high above. Several years before, the Greater London Council had begun a programme of grouting the junctions of prefabricated concrete panels on flats at Thamesmead which leaked water into tenants' flats. Fires at old people's homes in England and a school in France constructed in the CLASP system (designed originally for schools) brought about new regulations for fire prevention. In the USA glass fell out of skyscraper office blocks and rusting steel showered surrounding buildings for several years.

The list of failures, with each new addition widely publicised in the media, is a long one. Some older materials, notably concrete, began to fail as well. Calcium chloride, a rapid setting agent for concrete, turned out to corrode reinforcing bars if conditions were damp and if too much had been thrown into the concrete mix in the first place. It was discovered that high alumina cement, when builders put in too much water, underwent a process of conversion after a number of years in humid environments; after a set of spectacular failures, large numbers of buildings came under the suspicion of structural inadequacy and others had to be either permanently propped-up or partly reconstructed.

At the beginning of 1979 the weekly *Building Design* surveyed around sixty local authorities.[21] They reported planned or current repairs to post-war housing in their control to a value of around £200 million. Work included recladding ten-year-old tower blocks, demolishing two-storey steel system buildings, bonding cavity walls suffering tie fatigue, repairing structural cracks in five-year-old houses, and almost universally repairing leaking walls and roofs. Not all of this sample was entirely due to poor design or workmanship, for local authorities were themselves guilty of not adequately maintaining their housing stock.

This sample catalogue of specific disasters and the enormous sum of money involved was not entirely unanticipated for already the architectural profession had turned its attention to more tried and true methods of construction and materials in a sharp reaction against the post-war tradition of innovation in architectural design.

The profession

It would be too dramatic to suggest that the profession of architecture in Britain became a disaster area in the seventies. But its self confidence had been severely shaken by the catalogue of functional disasters from the late sixties, by the virulent popular press campaign against the profession and by what one of the most respected architectural academics, Patrick Nutgens, has described as 'the profession's erratic mania for self-flagellation and exposure. It published reports, for example on management, notifying the world of architects' notorious incompetence on costs and organisation, with indictments of their record. At the same time architects became more and more pre-posterous in their claims for attention. They set up as authorities on everything: on town planning . . . on landscape . . . on pollution . . . and on economics (to the utter amazement of economists who had, uncharacteristically, observed architects' inability to control costs)'.[22] Self-flagellation by architects was common in architectural papers throughout the decade and for a time during the mid-seventies took on the character of Chinese people's courts, where penitents denounced themselves before an audience of local cadres in an act of cleansing self-humiliation.

That was not enough, however, to stave off the major blow of the decade to the profession's self esteem—the Poulson affair. John Poulson, a Yorkshire architect, had corrupted a number of local authority officials and others and the lengthy trial which followed his exposure discredited the local political machine throughout the north east and occasioned close scrutiny of Westminster politicians' association with his various companies. In proper perspective it must be acknowledged that Poulson was merely one figure in a widespread network of small- and large-scale corruption in local government. But he was an architect and it was as the *architect* John Poulson that his name appeared in the sensational news coverage of the trial and in his subsequent bankruptcy hearings.

Alan Maudsley soon followed Poulson to jail in an unconnected corruption trial which served to reinforce public cynicism about the profession's image. Maudsley was not in private practice but was chief architect to Birmingham during much of that city's frenzied bid for eminence and prosperity during the sixties and early seventies. In the process Maudsley, who like all local authority architects had great power in influencing who got contracts and how certificates for work done were issued, succumbed to the financial blandishments of construction firms. Poulson and Maudsley were simply the first and best publicised of the list of corrupt architects. The lures of easy money and the pliability of council officials and politicians subsequently sent a small but significant number of architects to jail during the second half of the seventies. This hit harder than any other public exposure of the profession's failings. For it called into question the effectiveness of the profession both to police and to maintain its own integrity, and that at a time when the profession had anyway begun to undergo the throes of self-examination.

Architecture became an institutionalised profession in the mid-nineteenth century along with other professions like engineering and surveying which offered highly specialist knowledge and creative skills. An important element in the professional equation was the degree of personal trust, which went beyond the bounds of a legal contractual relationship, and involved the professional in a direct personal liability for his actions. The formal establishment of professions was brought about by the formation of associations with rules governing professional behaviour, minimum standard fees and financial independence from other related activities in the construction industry which might be seen to influence their judgement. Most of these associations were subsequently given royal charters and, in the thirties, the name architect was protected under an act of parliament.

Despite these outward signs of respectability (and it is a respectability which is closely related to social status) architects have always been slightly paranoid about their standing in the eyes of the world. Poulson, Maudsley *et al* demonstrated that members of the profession were as susceptible to commercial pressures as any tradesman: the image of the gentleman architect was simply a myth.

Britain has probably the largest *per capita* population of practising architects in the world. All 25,000 or so of them are registered with the Architects' Registration Council of the United Kingdom, the official body which polices professional conduct and the provisions of the Architect's Registration Act. Many of the total number belong to the Royal Institute of British Architects, membership of which is normally confused in the public mind with formal qualification to practice. But nearly half of the total are civil servants and another twenty per cent are salaried employees in private architectural practices. In the old nineteenth-century sense these architect-employees are not professionals, for they are not directly responsible to their clients. That fact is of particular relevance because the public and internal self-image of the profession and its codes are predicated on the old nineteenth-century pattern of independent private practice.

It makes sense for the large group of salaried architects who make up seventy per cent of the total number to maintain the myth of an occupation which has the status of an independant profession and firm corporate roots going back to the last century. But because they are not directly dependent on fee income and because their principals, and not they, are responsible to clients, or in public service not contractually responsible to anybody in particular, there is a clear line of demarcation between the two sorts of architect. In the seventies it has come out into the open with the formation within the Royal Institute of British Architects of the Association of Consulting Architects—who are all in private practice—and of the Salaried Architect's Group. Both organisations are respectful of the RIBA because its suffix on notepaper is still useful to impress clients and future employers, but the myth of a homogenous profession has begun to be questioned openly as salaried architects begin to realise that the RIBA and its codes and rules and private practice orientation is largely irrelevant in protecting their conditions of employment. It is unlikely however that much of this will appear on the public surface for private practitioners need the political weight of a numerically strong RIBA and salaried architects need the status which it confers. Nevertheless small groups of architects have broken away from the RIBA or have never joined it: in 1978 forty per cent of architects under thirty were not members. Both the almost defunct Architects' Revolutionary Council and the growing New Architecture Movement have attracted wide publicity within the architectural press and have exerted some influence on the counsels of the Architects' Registration Council, to which, as registered architects rather than as RIBA members, they are entitled to belong. It is doubtful if the Poulson affair was particularly influential on the formation of these and other small special interest groups within the profession. But Poulson and Maudsley and the others gave credence to existing uncertainties about the role of the architect and his professional organisation.

At the same time the commercial pressures of the post-oil-crisis slump caused some architects to re-evaluate the traditional ethical postures of the profession. Formerly deeply committed to the independence of the architect from all other activities in the construction industry and to maintaining a non-commercial approach to practice, the RIBA council, dominated by the private practitioner group, voted in 1977 to allow architects to advertise their services. Spurred on by the results of a survey conducted by the magazine *Building Design* it hastily reversed its decision. Apart from the expected opposition from the small group of old guard gentleman-style architects, salaried architects saw this move in the direction of commercialism as threatening the blanket professional status under which they thrived. Several months later a Monopolies Commission report ruled that minimum fees, one of the bulwarks of professional bodies against cut-price competition, were against the public interest. By the end of the year serious consideration was unofficially being given to following the American and Australian pattern of allowing architects to become developers. Other forms of limited financial liability were discussed as court decisions increased architects' responsibility for negligence and as the number of insurance companies prepared to provide professional indemnity fell (unlike doctors or lawyers, architects are always ready to testify against each other in law suits) and indemnity insurance premiums began to rise beyond the means of small- and medium-sized practices.

More damaging to professional self-esteem and potentially damaging to the traditional rôle of the architect as controller of building contracts has been the rise of the quantity surveyor. Virtually unknown outside Britain, the profession of quantity surveying has taken over several areas of the British architect's traditional functions, both in estimating the amount of work done during the progress of a contract, for which the builder is paid in stages, but also in advising at the preliminary design stage. The existence of quantity surveyors in Britain has produced a vicious circle in which architects, having gratefully relieved themselves of the tedious parts of their function, are now virtually without any training on the subject of costs and find themselves heavily reliant on a profession which is promoted as an exact science, with the attendant paraphernalia of precise bills of quantities and cost estimates. As any European or American architect will point out, the subject of building costs is not an exact science but an art. British architects who have largely given up this art now commonly find themselves on large commercial contracts landed not only with their own quantity surveying advisors but quantity surveyors privately retained by their clients to keep a distrustful eye on their design proposals. Most British architects have no experience of working abroad and so are hardly aware of the invidious position into which they have allowed themselves to fall.

More obviously erosive of the architect's traditional rôle has been the emergence of the 'design and build' contract. Under this system an entrepreneur negotiates or tenders not only to construct a building for a client, but to design it as well. Invariably architects are employed to carry out the design work, but in the execution of the work it is their employer rather than they who have the ultimate say in decisions on the quality of work and whether the building and its parts actually meet the original specification. In practice building is an extremely imprecise and negotiable affair. Apart from producing a consistently banal standard of architecture, design and build contracts have largely been conducted with as much propriety as contracts in which the architect is the unambiguous final arbiter. But for the professional *amour propre*, design and build represents a growing threat.

The end of the seventies saw the corporate profession in a state of great uncertainty about its rôle and function, demoralised by its legacy of failure to deliver any of the promised goods of the sixties and shrouded by the cloud of corruption of the early and mid-seventies. The future which it faces is uncertain. What is reasonably clear is that the voice of salaried architects is likely to be heard more frequently in its internal counsels. It is also clear that although this group represents young and radical architects, it has a vested interest in maintaining the *status quo* of the profession's public image. Perversely it will be private, traditionally conservative architects who are likely to bring about any structural changes in the way architects practise.

Part Two

RESPONSES

Alternatives

The crisis of confidence in architecture came later for the established profession than for young architects and students. During a period in the late sixties, especially at the time of worldwide student unrest, young designers had become so disgusted with what they saw as the megalomaniac pretentions and the overly expressive form of establishment Brutalist architecture that they retreated into a form of architectural-scientificism. Fuelled by the writings of Christopher Alexander[23] and others on design methodology they sought a basis for design which was devoid of the personal architectural tricks and foibles practised by their elders. Design methodology purported to bring all the elements of an architectural problem together in a mechanistic and therefore 'objective' way. For several years until Alexander recanted his system because of its impossible complexity and the difficulty of actually giving objective weightings to elements in the 'scientific' design equation, it was unfashionable in architecture schools to mention the word design or to discuss such notions as style or composition, on the grounds that these had put architecture into its current alienating position. In true architecture, the argument ran, good design came about as the natural outcome of logically following through the programme of a building. Such was the complexity of this task that students, not surprisingly, became obsessed with the process and not the product.

By the time Alexander had recanted, the anti-expressive design movement had anyway begun to take a new direction. This time it was towards the truth and directness of primitive building and technology exemplified in such books as Bernard Rudofsky's photographic studies of primitive settlements, *Architecture Without Architects*[24] and, in Britain, articles in the *avant garde* magazine *Architectural Design* on third-world urban squatter settlements—and more significantly in the form of Drop City, the paradigmatic built form of twentieth-century western primitivist architecture.

Designed and built by a group of people who had dropped out of materialistic American society, Drop City was constructed from the detritus of industrial civilization—mainly flattened car bodies—and put together in a way which suggested the highly sophisticated geometry of geodesic structures. Its importance was that it was not a third-world settlement nor the product of impoverished peasants dislocated from their land, but of people who had rejected the comfortable life of the high technology West. It was the model for many similar drop-out communities in the USA which were duly chronicled by the new alternative press in the form of cookbooks on dome geometry and construction, handbooks on self-sufficiency and such publications as the *Whole Earth Catalog*,[25] a polygot collection of tools, goods, books and equipment available through the enormous US mail order network. All the items in the *Catalog* were specifically useful in making the alternative life style possible: books on how to build log cabins, walking boots, gardening equipment, natural childbirth methods and so on. The *Catalog's* brief preface spoke in visionary terms of the coming into existence of a new realm which would develop 'intimate personal power . . . [the] power of the individual to conduct his own education, find his own inspiration, shape his own environment'.

In many respects this was no more than a revamping of the American ideal of the self-sufficient backwoodsman who had appeared in primitivist American literature from Thoreau through Walt Whitman to Walt Disney and Davy Crockett. But at the time it was seen as a realistic way of getting back to more fundamental and truthful patterns of living. There was a degree of hard-edged realism in not abandoning contemporary society completely but deliberately selecting from the goodies available in high consumer, high technology society those which were useful and which were low in technological content.

On the other side of the Atlantic, Britain's closed and highly regulated society presented formidable obstacles to any large-scale attempt at emulating the American alternative experience. There were not the wild, open spaces, there was the inimical climate and there were planning regulations which made it difficult for even establishment architects to build very much. In Britain the architectural implications of alternative low technology tended to be worked out in schools of architecture and, apart from the refurbishment of country barns and cottages, in models and theory rather than real life.

But with the oil price crisis and what was promoted in the media as the 'energy crisis', public attitudes changed overnight. By 1976 central government had begun to be interested in the possibilities of alternative energy sources: wave power, tidal power, wind power and solar power. But although it provided small sums of money for research projects the government soon began to learn to live with high oil prices (especially when it began to sell oil from its own wells in the North Sea) and little may be expected in the future in the way of public money. Preliminary results of research have so far been unspectacular. But in the schools of architecture a great deal of interesting design and research had been taking place from the early seventies onwards. In

1970 Alex Pike began work with a team at Cambridge on the design of
an autonomous house. It incorporated a number of low-energy features
such as solar heating, a sewage digestor, wind generator, heavy
adjustable insulation heat store, and indoor garden. However, it did not
get beyond the model stage.

At around the same time at the Polytechnic of Central London Steven
Szokolay, against the conventional wisdom that British skies were too
overcast for solar energy to be a viable proposition, set up a series of
computer studies and designed and installed a solar unit in a house at
Milton Keynes, with government backing. This was the first of a
number of small-scale test runs by local authorities, and notably the
Wates building group, but it is still thought to be too early to make sage
predictions about the commercial good sense of solar energy, although
the number of small manufacturers (not a few of them cowboys)
offering solar water-heating systems has risen rapidly. No British solar
heating system can provide heating all the year round and the financial
viability of any installation depends on the likely length of occupancy
of a house and the projected payback period. With a national average
occupancy of any house in the private sector of around seven years and
the fact that the behaviour of any system is still uncertain, even
supplementary solar heating remains at the experimental stage in
Britain.

One rare building which can probably be accepted, in an honorary
fashion, into the alternative canon is Arthur Quarmby's own house in
the small Yorkshire village of Holm. An early innovator in experimen-

Arthur Quarmby: Underground house, Holm, Yorkshire, 1976—rather too styled-up inside to belong properly to the brown rice Alternative canon

tal grp moulding design, Quarmby was faced with the problem of how to build a house in the green belt of the Pennines. His solution, often mooted in student designs over the last few decades, and nearly brought to reality in Archigram's abortive 1969 design for an entertainment facility in Monaco, was to build underground. Encircling a glass-roofed pool, the rooms on the downhill side of the house look out over the view and on the uphill side are either mechanically ventilated or face onto the pool. Highly insulated by the surrounding earth and heated partly by the warm pool in the middle, the internal climate has turned out to be stable and relatively cheap to maintain.

The Quarmby house is too sophisticated inside to belong to the alternative aesthetic of non-design, especially when it is compared with the buildings at Britain's major centre for alternative technology. The National Centre for Alternative Technology is located in a Welsh slate quarry. In operation since 1973, it comprises a small village of self-build houses, into which are incorporated a wide variety of cheap self-sufficient energy and living systems on long-term test. The director, Roderick James, is an architect and a number of architectural students have been active in setting up the community. Financed by a tourist board grant and entry fees from 60,000 visitors each year, it represents the only serious British parallel to the American self-sufficiency ideal. The difference is that it has had to adopt an institutionalised form and a commercial tourist packaging in order to make investigations into the simple life viable.

Beyond these instances British architects have not responded in any significant way to the challenge of dwindling world resources. There was applause for late seventies' government regulations which demanded much higher insulation standards in buildings; there was a forlorn official RIBA campaign in 1972 about 'long life, loose fit, low energy' as new principles of design and the slightly unrealistic suggestion from *The Architects' Journal* that people should wear more clothes and turn their heating down. (The unit 'clo' had been introduced with perfect seriousness by one of its technical writers to denote the thermal unit of one person in the nude.) Some architects imagined that the new exigent circumstances of high energy costs might generate a new low technology architectural aesthetic; perversely, for that point of view, it has turned out that folksy 'low technology' vernacular styles of the later seventies are based almost purely on picturesque *visual* composition. It has been the hard-edged, high technology stylists who have taken the issues of high insulation, minimal use of materials and loose fit to their hearts.

Housing

The failure of confidence in sixties' housing policy and practice—
tower blocks, large-scale redevelopment, vandalism, tenant dissatisfac-
tion, building failures and, worst, an undiminished housing waiting
list—led a number of architects and writers to look beyond the
discredited conventional architectural solutions of the sixties.

It was well enough known that the standard response of tenants when
questioned about their ideal dwelling was to describe a cottage with a
garden. Apart from viewing this as an idea above the ordinary council
tenant's station, such a solution seemed to architects and councillors to
be impossible given the economics of public housing. But it was a
solution ably and passionately argued in 1973 by the architectural
historian and broadcaster Nicholas Taylor, in his book *The Village in the
City*.[26] The book was a compound of history, which purported to show
that cottage building was part of a great British domestic tradition, and
of denunciation of megalomaniac redevelopment, tower blocks and
high density—and the *Ville Radieuse* theory on which they were
founded. Taylor's argument was for a density of around 80 persons to
the acre, family houses on the ground in 'neat little terraces of town
houses with small gardens, sufficient to house all . . . decently'.

The vision of small houses and small gardens was a seductive one.
Approval of gardens squared with research studies on vandalism by
the American sociologist Oscar Newman who in his *Defensible Space*[27]
of 1972 argued that vandalism on large housing estates was closely
connected with the absence or presence of territorial spaces around
buildings. Where there were no private or semi-private spaces or
'domains', casual vandalism could be expected more frequently than
where a clearly private domain existed, whatever its size. This was
translated by British housing theorists into a need for front porches,
back yards and gardens and individually identifiable (and if possible
personalised) dwellings.

By the end of the seventies the vision was in some cases coming true,
not least in the London Borough of Lewisham where Nicholas Taylor
had become chairman of the council planning committee. Howell Killik
Partridge Amis's Somerville Road scheme embodies most of Taylor's

ideas: small-scale family dwellings of no more than three storeys, small
back gardens, unostentatious and familiar—almost suburban—house
forms and a density of around 80 people to the acre. Somerville Road
was by no means the first of such schemes, for Taylor's passionate
vision of the village in the city had caught the imagination of local
authority planning committees. Their architects, even if they had been
thinking along the same lines, (and a number had), were now issued
with firm historical precedents, a credible summary of the extant quasi-
sociological position and good emotive reasons for building small
houses with gardens rather than tower blocks.

If the grand strategy and supporting philosophy of late seventies'
housing policy was neatly predicted in Taylor's book, other people
including architects thought the problems of bad modern housing were
outside the influence of building form or arrangement and more to do
with the relationship between the tenant/occupier, his housing and the
designer.

Tenant involvement

The most publicised attempt at directly involving tenants in their
housing was at Swinbrook Road in London's apallingly depressed
North Kensington. Spurred on by the conspicuous neglect of the area
by the rich borough of Kensington and Chelsea, a local community
action group went over the council's head and approached the Greater
London Council. It hoped to persuade the GLC to take over the area and
redevelop it. Somewhat to the local group's surprise the then Tory
administration agreed and a committee representing local people, the
borough, the GLC and GLC architects was set up to work out the broad
planning strategy and the fine-grain detail. Local interest and
enthusiasm ran high; preliminary surveys and questionnaires evoked an
astonishing 93 per cent response rate (40 per cent being the average
figure for this kind of thing). They revealed that most people wanted to
remain in the area, and were anxious that the estate should have a small
friendly character with doors on to the street, small gardens and the
possibility of personalisation. The final design more or less follows the
old street pattern with barrier blocks against the railway which runs
down one side of the site and the Westway motorway which runs down
another.

As with any attempt at involving local people and future tenants
there was the problem of the very long time elapsing between design
and completion—it is difficult to sustain local interest at a sufficient
pitch for the three to four years involved. By the time the scheme was
half complete it was reckoned that only 35 per cent of the original
inhabitants would return to the Swinbrook area; there had anyway
developed a fundamental split in the local community on racial lines.

Not entirely surprisingly GLC architects, who had spent enormous
amounts of unpaid time in the area for several years, subsequently
opted on other sites for what is euphemistically known as consultation:

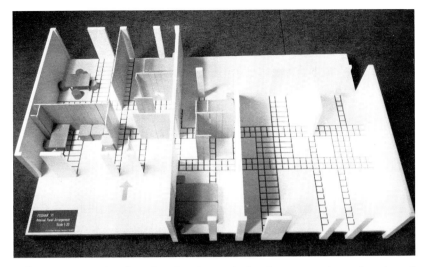

Greater London Council architects' department: PSSHAK model ready for clients. The grids indicate the relatively constrained limits of tenant decisions about panel and wall locations.

information is circulated to local people in the area to be redeveloped and they are asked to comment on a public exhibition of the architects' and planners' proposals. Some notice is then taken of their views. This is not however very different from what has become standard practice in ordinary planning enquiries run by local authorities and the Department of the Environment.

Slightly earlier, the GLC had been looking at ways of getting around the problem of designing for the unknown client. In 1970 two students at the Architectural Association, Nabs Hamdi and Nick Wilkinson, presented a student housing proposal to an audience which included the then Minister of Housing and the chief architect for GLC housing, Kenneth Campbell. It was based on the writings of the Dutch architect Nicholas Habraken who over the decade after 1961, when he had published *De Dragers en den Mensen* (published in translation by the Architectural Press as *Supports: an alternative to mass housing*)[3] had argued that the architect's function was to provide the basic infrastructure of structure, service runs and circulation. The future occupier would then go to a selection centre and order the various parts of his new house 'off the peg' rather as he might buy a suite of furniture. The final appearance of the building, both inside and out, would depend entirely on the client's choice. Since it presupposed a housing components industry (and as much choice as there is in say household goods) the occupier could, when he tired of one arrangement or façade, trade the old in, rearrange the internal partitions, and end up with a new dwelling—but still within the original structure.

Habraken's vision of supports was essentially megastructural— great structures striding across the countryside—and was not particularly concerned with the surrounding environment. But it represented the possibility of choice. Taken on board by the GLC, Hamdi and Wilkinson developed the system known as PSSHAK— Primary Supports Structure Housing Action Kit—which has been tried out on two small London sites. PSSHAK as an inevitably watered-down, anglicised version of the original has turned out to be simply the involvement of the future tenants in arranging room divisions (using models of the final moveable partition system) within a shell of pre-designed external walls, floors and pitched roofs. Further constraints were imposed by having to establish the location of service runs before the tenants decided on their layouts—which anyway were carefully guided by the architects.

The median between total participation and mere consultation is well represented by Ralph Erskine's work at Byker (illustrated on page 138). A run-down suburb of Newcastle-upon-Tyne, Byker formed a distinct and close-knit community—unlike many other areas where the much-used word community often simply means people living in one area. In mid-1969 Erskine set up his planning team in an old funeral parlour in the middle of Byker and opened up his drawing office to the locals, who were encouraged to discuss their needs and to watch the scheme develop on the drawing boards.

After his structure plan had been approved by local people and the local authority, Erskine was appointed architect for the scheme and the first houses were put up. The tenants who moved in were canvassed for views about the success of their dwellings and their views about improvements were incorporated into the next phase, and the same process continued with subsequent phases. Tenants are reckoned to be very satisfied with the new Byker—largely because the designers are physically *seen* to be responding to suggestions and complaints. Equally important is the way in which the local housing team has developed a policy of involving future tenants in the choice of their new accommodation and in explaining what it will be like. Few local authorities do this and most inform their new tenants only a few weeks before they are scheduled to move in. The Byker local authority housing team starts the process some six or nine months beforehand, which allows tenants time to order furniture and fittings and save up for them in good time. In addition they maintain a highly sophisticated social-work approach to what in the hands of other local authorities is merely an administrative routine. Although tenants can indeed make comments and see designs evolve in the drawing office, that advice and those drawings are for the next phase of the whole scheme and do not relate to their own dwellings. In practice much of the initial local enthusiasm has faded away despite architects' and housing officers' continued commitment to the idea of close involvement and consultation.

Despite the Byker architects' attempts to design for future tenants' wants and needs, their approach has been essentially amateur in the sense that it relied on chance meetings with those local people who had bothered to think about and then express their attitude to their dwelling. But its relative success has encouraged other architects to dabble in the same form of preliminary discussion in pubs and local meeting halls, usually carried out with an even greater degree of haphazardness and amateurism. However, it has the useful political function of enabling the architects to point to their practical concern for designing to local taste.

Ahrends Burton and Koralek's procedure at Chalvedon, Basildon, was rather made professional. The practice brought in a sociologist to assess the first stage of this large housing scheme at Basildon. Peter Ellis's surveys into tenant satisfaction with houses already built greatly influenced the layout and details of succeeding stages. Untypically, Ellis claimed that sociology can be used as a predictive tool, although this is more likely to be the case with very large housing schemes which are designed and built in stages so that there is the possibility of feedback from early stages.

Surveys of this sort are expensive and only a practice with Ahrends Burton and Koralek's conviction about their usefulness is likely to spend part of its hard-earned fees in such a way. However, for more economically minded designers there is HAK, a Housing Action Kit, designed and introduced by the GLC and the Department of the Environment, which is intended as a cheap do-it-yourself survey of tenant attitudes and preferences. It contains reasonably neutral questions (difficult to devise), which can be easily processed and later interpreted even by laymen—which, as far as statistical interpretation is concerned, architects effectively are.

Most of these cases of tenant consultation have involved simulating, to some degree or other, the sort of relationship which exists between a private architect and his client. Local authority housing has traditionally been standardised in the name of visual and architectural continuity and unity, and on the grounds of economy. But at the end of 1978 the London Borough of Bromley embarked on a small pilot scheme in which prospective tenants were each allocated an architect to design their new house in the real-life pattern of private practice. Bromley argued that the cost would not be significantly higher than designing a similar look-alike estate and anyway that the gains to the local environment would be worth any additional cost. If the scheme works it will be applied to larger estates. Given the underemployment of local authority architects at the end of the seventies it may seem an attractive approach to other local authorities.

Community housing practices
Halfway outside the sphere of official architectural practice, a number of young architects have turned towards the idea of community architecture. This has been centred mainly on refurbishment rather than new building. Some schemes have been relatively successful. At Black Road in Macclesfield the architect Rod Hackney mobilised his neighbourhood into refurbishing its dwellings (subsequently with official support and finance) after he had discovered that the area was designated for comprehensive redevelopment. Since then he has found himself, almost involuntarily, involved with other self-help groups of

tenants and housing groups throughout the country. Chris Whittaker, a partner in an otherwise conventional practice, has become a kind of roving expert witness in planning enquiries—on the side of local people faced with the steamroller of local authority redevelopment. Other groups of architects have become involved in long-term grass-roots work with local communities, often acting as community workers as much as architects. In Glasgow, a group of young architects known as ASSIST has to some extent supplanted local authority architects in providing an alternative architectural service for local residents and housing associations. In Covent Garden a small community architecture group has begun the low-cost refurbishing of shops and dwellings which the GLC machine had maintained were too expensive to do anything with.

The notion of community architectural practice is analogous to contemporary citizens' advice bureaux and community law centres, which are run by professionals who deploy their specialisms in the service of ordinary people—people whose voices would otherwise be unheard in the secretive confabulations of British bureaucracy. Even the official architects' body, the Royal Institute of British Architects, has recognised the virtues of this kind of practice and has set up a community architecture working group—though there is more than a suspicion that its establishment was related to the Institute's concern that young architects were beginning not to renew their subscriptions. By using the classic tactic of assimilation, as one critic put it, the RIBA had developed 'liberal antibodies in the shape of the working group to fight off the radical threat'.

In addition to tenant participation there have been a small number of attempts to involve future tenants in building their own housing. Politicians of the new centre left pointed out that the old Labour Party dream was not of housing the population in state-owned dwellings but providing everybody with his own home, and around 1975–6 official Labour policy veered towards the idea of selling council accommodation, thus falling in line with the practice of many Conservative local authorities, though not necessarily their underlying social theory. At the same time the GLC had begun to experiment with methods of tenure which allowed tenants to take a stake in the ownership of their housing by paying a combined rent/mortgage repayment, and one or two schemes started in which housing co-operatives were given derelict property to refurbish themselves, with grants and materials provided by the council. At the end of this refurbishment the council and the co-operatives were to enter into a joint tenure arrangement which would eventually lead to the property being owned by the co-operative.

Slightly outside the official housing programme have been several attempts at council-funded private self-build schemes designed by the architect Walter Segal. These have either involved full council mortgages or an equity-sharing scheme with the local authority. Segal's system is more to do with assembling standard building components than with building. Segal himself orders the materials in order of assembly: timber, plasterboard, gravel and concrete. With the aid of a manual which is also both the specification *and* the material order list, the owner/builder puts the house together with the aid of not much more than standard do-it-yourself electric power tools. Practically no skills are required and, equally important, each person puts up his own house rather than having to help put up other houses before his own is started (as is the case with most co-operative ventures). Segal's system has one drawback: it relates entirely to a timber, orthogonal, slightly Modern Movement aesthetic of flat roofs and post and beam construction. Builder-owners have little choice of style, and the Segal style does not always find favour with planners.

Local authority architects and housing authorities are reluctant to become involved in too much self-help, equity sharing or tenant involvement beyond a token consultation. It is partly a matter of inertia in the face of the unfamiliar, partly because the existence of such alternative approaches to housing indicates that the bureaucratic machine is inadequate, and partly because they involve civil servants in a great deal of work attending meetings after hours, working up local trust and enthusiasm and in guiding the inevitably inexperienced participants through the maze of official procedures.

Housing without architects

The notion that architects had a limited or even no rôle to play in housing gained currency throughout the seventies. This notion was implicit enough in government recommendations, notably in 1978, that local authorities should use design and build contracts in favour of more expensive architect-designed and supervised schemes. But for the profession it took the explicit form of a series of public denunciations by one Conrad Jamieson.[28] Widely published and read around 1975–6, Jamieson's argument was that 'popular housing is not really the architect's proper business or concern'. His view (probably not uninfluenced by the fact that his father was a developer in the USA) was that there was no point in architects spending time designing housing when a whole repertoire of plans, external detailing and construction was readily available to the builder. 'Even up to the last War, most architects would have asked why ordinary house forms should be designed afresh when, with minor modifications, designs copied from traditional pattern books would do better or at least as well.' Arguing that the days of large-scale redevelopment were anyway over and that most new housing would be located on small infill sites or take the form of refurbishment, his view was that the use of standard pattern book designs, of the sort promoted by the Scottish Housing Authority and by the GLC (though not much used by the latter) was all that was needed—architects were unnecessary. Given the relatively ineffectual performance of housing architects since the war, Jamieson's view is a seductive one. If his prediction of a housing glut in the next decade is accurate, it may well come true. But it is an argument which is fundamentally based in the class-war attitude to public housing, seeing it as a necessary part of the fabric of British society which however is not sufficiently up-market to warrant the attention of a highly skilled profession. It is also an argument which would, if applied rigorously, deprive public housing of the social and visual benefits which a small number of architects have been able to give to the British housing scene.

Neovernacular

The most prevalent consequence of the agonies of post tower block *triste* has been the emergence of a new style in housing—'neovernacular'. First used as a joking pejorative by this author, the label has now, like Gothic and Baroque (originally terms of abuse) been shyly adopted into common parlance by the practitioners of this patronisingly sentimental approach to housing design. Neovernacular pretends to be a response to what tenants are thought to want or admire. It is entirely concerned with what houses look like on the outside.

By the end of the seventies its standard characteristics had firmed up: pitched, ostensibly slated roofs; brick walls with nooks and crannies wherever possible and irregular forms and perimeters; weatherboarded or tile-hung upper floors; porches, oriels, bays and dormers; irregular groupings of houses usually based on a modified version of the Radburn layout (discussed below); and dwellings never more than two or three floors in height.

It is promoted by its practitioners for its directness and honesty of form and detailing, for its ordinariness and absence of overtly architectural styling; for its supposed grass roots connections with the everyday building of a (long dead) rural village England; and on the grounds that it is not high rise. Housing estates in the style have regularly been awarded prizes in recent annual housing awards and it is demanded by many local and central government housing committees; in one county at least it has been enshrined and made virtually mandatory in a notorious planning document, the Essex design guide.

The arcadian ideal
The exemplary Neovernacular housing estate is still Palace Fields at Runcorn new town, the first phase of which was completed in 1973. Made up of dark brown brick dwellings and garages with plastic slate-covered monopitched roofs, it is organised in what at first glance appears to be a casually disordered array around a series of *culs de sac*. Now that the dense planting has grown up it has acquired the village character which the designers originally had in mind.

Runcorn Development
Corporation Architects: Palace
Fields, 1972

The air of casualness is achieved partly by planting and partly by the irregular disposition of (otherwise standard) dwellings and garages in pairs and groups around the edge of the tarmac miniature village 'greens' of the *culs de sac*. Non-standard brick and tarmac road surfaces and brick and grass verges have been introduced in a way which disobeyed then mandatory highway engineers' rules about curbings, road widths, surfaces and footpaths, but which in practice allowed ready access for the service vehicles around whose manoeuvering dimensions the rules were supposedly formulated. Ground surfaces, planting and buildings read all of a designed piece, and the *culs de sac* have in practice been turned into informal spaces where children play, local inhabitants talk and walk and the occasional slow-moving car nudges its way in to park outside a back door or in one of the miniature barn-style garages. Subject of fierce highway regulation committee argument at the time, the *culs de sac* at Palace Fields have been illustrated as exemplars in recently revised suburban road suggestions from the Department of the Environment.[29] Roads apart, Palace Fields is noteworthy for the unity of its design and for its transformation of the standard Radburn layout from a diagrammatic ideal into a cosy informal village arrangement.

71

Radburn

Radburn planning and Neovernacular are made for each other—although that was not the original intention when Clarence Stein and Henry Wright introduced the layout in 1929 in a speculative housing scheme at Radburn, New Jersey. Based on groups of so-called superblocks of about 40 acres, each encircled by secondary roads off intra-town expressways and divided up by slow access roads with *culs de sac* off, it was predicated by a desire to separate traffic and pedestrians completely. Round each *cul de sac* were grouped clusters of twelve to fifteen houses at a density of twenty to thirty people per acre (average figures for current British housing are around 70 to 100 ppa). Separating the clusters of houses were meandering landscaped parks. Motor cars used the road network, pedestrians used a path network across the parks and through underpasses to schools and facilities in adjoining superblocks. Parks contained community recreation facilities and houses were planned with living rooms facing over private back gardens to the local park. Service rooms and entrances faced the *culs de sac*.

Used in various modified configurations in many of the British postwar new towns, Radburn represented the major alternative to the *Ville Radieuse* high-rise approach to estate planning, although in the hands of economically minded housing committees much of the landscaping and public areas (as was the case with high-rise schemes) were pared down or omitted.

However attenuated, Radburn's small scale, its association with one- or two-storied housing, its non-grid planning and its potential for transformation with only slight adjustment into cosy, organic English vernacular village-style planning, made it the perfect setting for houses designed in the Neovernacular style. In the hands of exterior designers as skilled as the Palace Field architects, the concatenation of style and

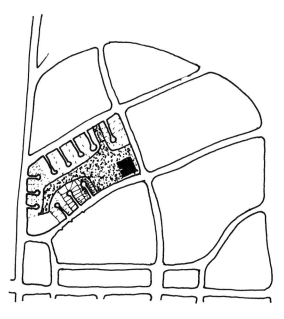

Sketch showing the original Radburn layout, with one of six superblocks detailed. Houses are arranged around the *culs de sac* off secondary roads. The central green (with a school or other community building) forms a private communal spine.

COUNTY COUNCIL OF ESSEX

layout could bring about as close an approximation to the instant arcadian housing vision as any architect is likely to get.

Neovernacular Radburn enshrined

Other architects were thinking along the same lines at the time and in the year of completion of the first major phase of Palace Fields (1973), architects of the Essex County Council persuaded their masters to put out the *Design Guide for Residential Areas*. It was aimed at rural housing developers who, in the eyes of the Essex architects, had begun to destroy the charm and integrity of too many rural Essex villages with banal 'unsympathetic' and often builder-designed housing for sale. It is not clear if it had occurred to the Essex architects that this kind of housing was itself a twentieth-century vernacular.

The *Guide* encouraged the use of the Radburn layout in its insistence that 'existing and proposed new residential areas shall, as far as is practicable, be separated from the main flow of through traffic' and mouthed conventional townscape wisdom to the effect that there should be diversity in densities. It insisted that individual dwellings be 'well designed' in terms of the visual composition of the surrounding area, which in practice required the observer to ignore all surrounding buildings later than around 1910; and required that they should be built from 'suitable materials', have care for the relationships between such things as the window shapes and sizes of adjoining buildings together with 'architectural detailing, used to reinforce the character required by the design and its location'.

The authors of these standard good-taste and vague architectural prescriptions had the grace to admit that 'what constitues good design has far too often been written off as a matter of opinion or taste' but they hoped by setting out a clearly related structure of layout and house design *policy* that better housing schemes and a greater consistency in the granting of planning permissions would result. In a mistaken attempt to clarify what were not much more than pious hopes, the authors appended drawn examples of good and bad housing design whose differences, to observers six years later, are difficult to distinguish from each other. Both seem to be in a somewhat Neovernacular style.

Architects who first applauded this attempt to formalise 'good' Neovernacular design in simple terms for unlettered builders and developers, suddenly found themselves having to toe the line with rather more exactitude than either they or almost certainly the authors of the *Guide* had intended. With similar guides put out by other counties, such as Cheshire, it quickly became, in the hands of planning control officers, a set of rigid design rules. But it has had many supporters even among the architectural fraternity, whose views are well summed up in a letter from an Essex architect to *Building Design* in 1977: 'The guide encourages the vernacular style and this strikes a responsive chord in the public mind to such an extent that "design guide" housing finds a ready market. If this is 'folksy' architecture then an advancement in housing design of an elitist nature must fail because the client, i.e. the public, does not want it'.

Apart from the proliferation of *non sequiters*, this passage is of interest because it is not untypical of the view of Neovernacularists— not all of whom, it should be said, necessarily feel that they themselves are in particular need of design guides. Of additional interest is the cheerful acceptance of the notion that Neovernacular is a *style*—rather than as many of its practitioners would really prefer to believe, a simple, straightforward way of doing architecture. That kind of self-deluding ingenuousness is an essential part of the baggage of Neovernacular.

At Palace Fields the monopitched roofs were supposed to be sympathetic to, or based on, local indigenous building. No real life examples have ever been produced in evidence—almost certainly because there are none. The monopitch roof, originally devised for mass housing as a complete prefabricated unit which was dropped on to the walls built on site, is probably an invention of GLC architects in the early sixties—and has its roots in Mediterranean peasant building which will be discussed later.

Ralph Erskine: Eaglestone,
Milton Keynes, 1975—affected
rusticity too frequently
repeated, and too arbitrarily
changed to deceive

The somewhat idiosyncratic roofs and the austerity of Palace Fields'
dark brown brickwork and detailing indicate the existence of
conscious design. Such subsequent designers as Ralph Erskine at
Milton Keynes' Eaglestone appear to have attempted to design out the
appearance of design. The self-evident absurdity of this can be clearly
seen in this developer-sponsored largely private housing scheme. A
collection of otherwise modest and conventional developer dwellings

Shankland Cox: Hayes Court, Hillingdon, 1978. A laboured attempt to create a sense of variety and a 'village' quality. In this case all the windows line up. 'Slates' are of plastic or composition material.

on a slightly hilly site, the appearance of their having been developed piece-meal is created by arbitrary changes in the colour of roof tiles and brickwork from one set of dwellings in a row to another. The appearance of non-architect-designed downmarket ordinariness is suggested by details such as projecting bow windows, rough wooden balconies, and whimsical folksy suburban timberwork. The appearance of having been comfortably lived in by a race of ardent build-it-yourselfers is broadly hinted at by the proliferation of large quantities of unplaned timber posts and frames, porches and balconies. All three techniques are to be found on Erskine's Byker housing megastructure at Newcastle where they are deployed with remarkable bravura and with some meaning. At Eaglestone they read merely as arbitrary cosmetic gestures in the direction of the vaguely self-build twentieth-century suburban end of Neovernacular.

Between Palace Fields and Eaglestone lies a morass of Neovernacular alternatives all aimed in the direction of ordinariness, and the grass roots of regional building, and desperately away from monumental tower-blockism. There are occasional side paths which architects follow in an attempt to imitate the way in which suburban dwellers personalise their own houses. Erskine used rough timbers, Shankland Cox in a group of housing schemes for the London borough of Hillingdon detailed otherwise standard terrace houses with contrasting external skins—one house in plain brick, another in painted brick, another in stucco, another in weatherboarding. To add a sort of verisimilitude to this otherwise patent sham (the structure behind is standard blockwork and timber) the designers have deliberately contrasted the size and shape of windows, roof pitches and the building line to produce a stage-set English vernacular village in the heart of fringe suburban London.

This relentless 'village' aesthetic has been imposed in the name of giving tenants a 'little nudge in the direction in which they might start to personalise their houses . . . if a tenant feels less intimidated by his surroundings by the absence of an overbearing aesthetic he may feel more at home'.[30] Which is to say that the architects hoped that the tenants liked the Neovernacular style more than the brick Brutalist or post-war Modern Movement or any other recent housing style, and suggests a movement back to the notion of architecture as social engineering, however gently designed.

Shankland Cox's pseudo-villages in Hillingdon are relatively small in scale, but at Bowthorpe on the outskirts of Norwich is the beginning of a vast Neovernacular housing scheme of three projected villages to be packed with 13,000 people when it is completed in the early 1980s. An unintentional museum of all the clichés of supposedly traditional Norfolk building, the pace of building has been forced and densities kept high in an entirely 'untraditional' way—for the ordinary twentieth-century reason that Norwich council bought the land at the peak of the property boom in 1973 and subsequently needed to keep interest losses on the undeveloped land as low as possible. An attempt was made at vernacularising standard dwellings by the use of irregular street layouts, contrasting cladding materials, dormers and the like, but by 1978 the scheme was so large in scale that the repertoire of Neovernacular tricks had been exhausted—it had been spread too thinly over too many buildings. Anybody taking seriously the architects' claim to have designed in the style of traditional Norfolk buildings would be puzzled by the real vernacular buildings around about.

Hack private and public architects who design what are little more than standard council houses with a few details which can only by a long stretch of the imagination be called local or traditional, regularly

Norwich Corporation architects' department: Bowthorpe village, Norwich, 1977

trot out the implausible proposition that they are designing in sympathy with local indigenous buildings. Their vernacular techniques are the use of bricks, roof pitches and occasionally window details such as reveals or lintels—all of which are to be found on some local buildings. When pressed however, they are rarely able to produce convincing evidence beyond a generalised gut feeling that there *is* a relationship with local vernacular, a feeling normally based on one or two strolls or motor-car tours in the area around the site.

That is not always the case. The Norwich-based firm of Feilden and Mawson has long been treading a delicately judged path between overt Neovernacularism and immaculately detailed brick Brutalism with a mediaeval twist, based to a large extent on Bernard Feilden's personal interest in old English architecture and his experience of restoration work on both York Minster and St. Paul's Cathedral. Describing a recent design for a small housing scheme at St. Columb Minor, the practice argued that this collection of irregularly disposed buildings lining a steep, winding back street in the town was based on 'building forms familiar to the Cornish scene . . . which appear sensitive and unassertive and above all Cornish'.[31] Despite the preliminary difficulty that the scheme is built in concrete blockwork with mass-produced tile roofs, Paul Oliver, the respected student of African vernacular building, has been able to identify sources for various elements of the design (which he pointed out in an otherwise favourable *Architects' Journal* review) which had 'been anthologised and used somewhat uncertainly': a back-street townscape based on local fishing towns, flights of steps from fishermen's cottages, garden walls of dry stone with turf cappings and the like. The flights of stairs are apparently inconvenient for babies, prams and washing but that is one of the prices of Neovernacular picturesqueness.

Similar Neovernacular anthologising mingled with straight vernacular reproduction is to be found in Essex County Council's Dutch Quarter at Chelmsford. In this conservation area building regulations were especially—and very unusually—relaxed so that the old mediaeval street lines and buildings could be copied. At Withyham, Sussex, concern that new houses for old people should fit in with local buildings obliged the architects to design a row of dwellings in a somewhat nineteenth-century *cottage ornée* manner, complete with porches and reproduction cast iron railings. The scheme attracted a special grant for building in real rather than imitation stone. So convincing at a first glance is this pastiche that what elsewhere is known as ordinary old people's housing is at Withyham described as almshouses. The nineteenth century has returned in more ways than one.

The catalogue of late-seventies Neovernacular mass housing is statistically impressive, even if the buildings on the ground are notable mainly for their close resemblance to thirties' council housing, with a little more in the way of landscaping. Dull, hack with a few tricks

Feilden and Mawson: St Columb Minor, 1978—attempt to create a fishing village impression in concrete blockwork.

attached, quasi-archaeological, highly wrought or semi-Disneyland, Neovernacular is the reigning style in mass housing. By the late seventies it is as inevitable for people on the housing lists as tower blocks were in the sixties and four-storey walk-ups in the fifties. Its exteriors may speak of anti-tower blockism, of a simple better life, of the hint, in the form of miniscule patches, of private gardens, and of a rugged 'honesty', but Neovernacular interiors are exactly the same as all other public housing interiors before it; the style offers tenants no new way of living. Neovernacular architects, who have spent much time breast-beating during the seventies about their former arrogance in forcing tower blocks on people, have not fundamentally changed their inner convictions that they know what people really should have in the way of housing. All that has changed is the style in which it is done.

Adjuncts to the instant village green

The Neovernacular style is normally a housing style but, given its current popularity, it is not entirely surprising that other building types get the same treatment. Buckinghamshire architects for example, under their former chief architect Fred Pooley, have been using it for a long time in school buildings. Their typical imitation farmyard-plus-barn character presumably goes back to Rousseauesque notions about the education of children among rural nature and there is probably some mileage in the idea of the *Kindergarten*—the place where children are grown and nurtured like flowers—or here, presumably, like cereal crops.

In and around the new town of Milton Keynes, schools have served a design propaganda function as well. Under the rules of British local government management, new town development corporations have no control over such community buildings as schools and day centres. This was particularly noticeable to mid-seventies visitors to Milton Keynes. Dotted amongst the regular and clear surfaces of the new town's *avant garde* housing estates were to be seen the sentinels of the new ancient values in the form of pitched 'slated' roofs, warm brickwork and higgledy-piggledy layouts of the primary and

Building Design Partnership: Town Hall, Tewkesbury, 1977—neovernacular on a large scale, but designed on a symmetrical layout.

Alfred Beck Centre

London Borough of Hillingdon architects' department: Alfred Beck Centre, Hillingdon, 1974

secondary schools designed by Bucks County Council architects. Centre piece for these strategically placed exemplars of anti-modernism was the Milton Keynes headquarters building. Designed before the corporation was completely organised, it was an early Neovernacular addition to an old building, complete with dramatic roofs and chunky brickwork. One of the first designs by the new corporation architects was a superbly detailed cool glass and steel addition, a gesture of defiance to the patronising sampler left behind for them to follow.

Nowhere in Britain could the early battle lines of the opposing architectures of the hard edge and the soft centre be more clearly seen than in Milton Keynes. But by the end of the decade the Bucks legacy had triumphed. Most expressive of this is Neath Hill, an estate in the northern area of the town which now nudges its double loops of Radburn-based, neo-Hampstead-Garden-Suburb vernacular housing obsequiously into the base of a local community school centre in the mature rural Bucks Neovernacular style.

At Tewkesbury in Gloucestershire the newly created council had its new town hall done in a proper 'vernacular' manner—a gauche collection of asbestos-substitute slate roofs and complicated interlocking forms which is ultimately and, given its Neovernacular pretensions, perversely, based on the strictest axial symmetry of plan. As is the case with Bowthorpe, the building is too extensive and too large in scale for its 'traditional' detailing to work in any way convincingly.

The Alfred Beck Centre at Hillingdon, Middlesex, is a similar case, where an essentially domestic style has been applied to a large building—here an all-purpose theatre complete with moving walls,

81

Robert Matthew Johnson-
Marshall: Civic Centre,
Hillingdon, Middlesex, 1978

high technology theatre equipment, and a ceiling which is insulated against the noise of low flying jets. These late twentieth-century characteristics are curiously at odds with the Neovernacular materials—brick facings and substitute slate roofs—and complicated subsidiary farmyard forms arranged around the perimeter of the auditorium. Designed by the local borough architects, Alfred Beck pays deferential stylistic respect to the largest Neovernacular building in England—the Hillingdon town hall. From outside this consists of a grouping of expressive forms, highly wrought roofs, large square windows with intricate hand-made brick surrounds, all set on a great plinth enclosing an underground car park, which is lit by a monumental range of brick arches. It looks rather like a small orderly hill town and that seems to be a view acceptable to the architects. Designed by Robert Matthew Johnson-Marshall & Partners, it has been described as a mingling of the shingle style with Swiss chalet. Baillie Scott, Norman Shaw, Robert Venturi and Richardson & Wright have all been summoned up by bemused critics as possible sources. The architects themselves claim that Hillingdonians have an affection for 'the vernacular, nostalgic overtones of the English village, kindly sloping roofs . . . and above all human scale!'. Their new civic centre is 'an attempt to acknowledge this need for friendliness in architecture without sacrificing in any way the requirements of functional efficiency and sensible economy ... which speaks a language intelligible to its users'. In fact per occupant it is the most expensive civic centre to be built in Britain and at the time the architects had embarked on a singularly experimental internal layout and organisation which they could hardly have guaranteed would produce functional efficiency (one route is a quarter of a mile long). Based on a central vertical circulation core the office floors are located at half levels around it, although that is far from obvious from outside.

The most recent phase of building at Hillingdon town hall has involved adding a small bell tower, salvaged from the old town hall, to one of the roofs and incorporating into the new a set of similarly salvaged wrought iron gates against which newly married couples have 'traditionally' been photographed in the past. New and old have been put together with the greatest earnestness though with little of the ethical seriousness which exposes the direct 'naturalness' of relationship between the form of a building and its actual internal arrangement.

Hillingdon town hall's façadism has been sufficiently impressive to

J. Sainsbury's architects' department: Store at Bowthorpe, Norfolk

Holder and Mathias: ASDA store, South Woodham Ferrers, Essex, 1978

Stanley Keen and Partners:
Housing at Fenn Farm, South
Woodham Ferrers, Essex, 1978

encourage followers. Two notable examples are a 'traditional Norfolk style' Sainsbury's supermarket in sub-Disneyland Bowthorpe and a bogus vernacular barn-style shopping centre at Woodham Ferrers, the village jewel in the *Essex Design Guide* diadem. Even the pro-Neovernacular *Architects' Journal* was disinclined to report more than the promoters' hope that its sloping roof might 'give the impression of a Victorian market hall rather than a present day superstore'. With a certain stylistic consistency Sainsburys at Bowthorpe have decided to sell ethnic-style hot bread baked on the premises.

These and the information centre on the Norfolk Broads designed by Feilden and Mawson in the form of a floating thatched cottage (whose secondary use is presumably to demonstrate Neovernacular to outlying Norfolk waterways communities) are from the hands of perfectly earnest designers. It is more worrying than ludicrous that designers should seriously attempt to create a fantasy world for sturdy peasants paying computerised rates bills, and doughty village goodwives pushing chrome trollies through ranges of goods nationally advertised on television towards the hot bread, fresh from stainless steel high-technology ovens. The patronising assumption that ordinary people live a life closer to that of Tolkien's Hobbiton than the exigent twentieth century; the stage-set decoration of timber truss and blockwork technology with fake slates and the most recently fashionable rustic cladding materials—these are not inconsistencies which disturb practitioners of the style. The simple reiteration of adjectives such as 'honest', 'humane', 'direct' and 'unpretentious' is enough for them. Yet if Neovernacular were any of these things at any more than a superficial cosmetic level, those inconsistencies would have exercised its protagonists to some degree. As it is, that kind of

Feilden and Mawson: Broadland
Conservation Centre, Norfolk
Broads, 1977

Illustration used in South
Woodham Ferrers publicity
brochures—seductive
architectural vision of fake
peasant life

debate of architectural morals is not encouraged: Astragal, the
Architects' Journal's backwoods commentator, put the 'lets not think
about it' position succinctly: 'Wasn't it the over-theoretical,
programmatic approach to some of the founding fathers that led to the
failure of much high rise, IB (industrial building) and the rest? . . . Let's
stick to trying to put up weatherproof building that people like'.

Recent models

It needs to be said that even the ludicrous end of late seventies'
Neovernacular has its origins in reasonably respectable fifties' and
sixties' arguments and attitudes. The seeds are to be found in fifties'
and sixties' visions of Italian hillside villages, New Empiricism,

Townscape and the simple life; and in one or two exemplary brick People's Detailing housing designs. Their pitched roofs, small windows, balconies, brickwork and occasional rendering and 'village' layouts were a gesture of solidarity with the spirit of proletarian vernacular village building—a spirit well typified by the cottage rows and walkups of the early Lansbury estates of 1951. Subsequently seen as related to the Scandinavian slide backwards out of the Modern Movement, known dismissively as the New Empiricism, the style was rejected in the late fifties by a younger generation of architects who favoured a styled-up international version of Modern Movement architecture. But not before it had reached a kind of apotheosis in the Smithsons' Sudgen House in Watford, of 1954. Never New Empiricists, who were considered not intellectually tough enough, the Smithsons had made a conscious effort to work within the vernacular of everyday speculator housing and (importantly at a time of great shortage in building materials) of available materials. Its deliberately awkward disposition of windows (brought about by locating them according to the function of the room they lit) brick walls, tiled roof and simple rectangular plan recommended the building to that part of the emerging Brutalist ethic who favoured a straightforward use of materials and a reduction to rough, primary forms. Whether intentional or not, it represented a styled-up, updated version of the 'vernacular' tendencies of People's Detailing.

Most subsequent brick Brutalist housing was a watered down version of Corb's Maison Jaoul, with exposed floor slabs separated vertically by panels of brickwork. But in small private houses of the late sixties, like those of Brett and Pollen at Christmas Common, Peter Aldington's own house at Turn End, Bucks, and Eric Lyons' Span development in New Ash Green, a small group of architects developed highly polished variants on the vernacular theme. These all ostentatiously paid respect to vernacular materials: brick and slate being most preferred; and to what were reckoned to be vernacular forms: the Brett and Pollen house was reminiscent of a water mill, Aldington's house of a Mediterranean farmyard, Neyland and Unglass's Harlow Casbah of a hill fort; but the exact genealogy of the others is, other than in a general way, less easy to pinpoint to any precise building type or locality. All of them however openly proclaimed their modernism in the form of big windows, the occasional exposed reinforced concrete slab, single pitch roofs (which were common in the Mediterranean but probably unknown in traditional British domestic vernacular) and inside, exposed and preferably unpainted timber beams and fittings. In most of these cases the folksiness was at a minimum. 'Free' planning, crisp detailing and stylishness, however deliberately gauche, was at a maximum. Critics of the Sugden house who objected to the Smithsons' attempt to do all this in the grammar of traditional domestic brick design (small windows, boxy rooms and so on), would probably have said much the same of these later examples.

Darbourne and Darke:
Lillington Gardens, Pimlico,
London (first stage), 1968

During the sixties these cool quasi-vernacular buildings were approved of but were uncommon. They could only be accepted into the reigning Brutalist canon as third cousins, for they did not carry enough of the required tough detailing nor were they normally on the monumental scale which typified mainstream Brutalism. Waiting in the wings as an example for mild-mannered brick Brutalists anxious to make a decent withdrawal from Brutalism's newly unpopular monumentalism—but without being seen to have ditched their convictions overnight—there was the work of Darbourne and Darke, and particularly their Lillington Gardens scheme in Pimlico, built between 1964 and 1972.

For architects making the transition from sub-Brutalist tower blocks, Lillington Gardens was almost paradigmatic. In contrast to the concrete-frame tower blocks of Churchill Gardens, the first two stages of Lillington Gardens were a tough, brick design, disposed in Italian hillside fashion along Vauxhall Bridge Road. Predominant features of the scheme are its balconies festooned with heavily planted foliage, small landscaped courtyards, hard brick landscaping complete with ramping, external stairways and half-private gardens enclosed by low walls in the dark brick favoured by the practice—and by Corb at Maison Jaoul, to which the scheme also pays homage in the exposed floor slab edges, canted balcony soffits and clear distinction between supporting wall and lightweight infill panel. The third stage, built under emerging Neovernacular influence and the introduction of

Darbourne and Darke:
Lillington Gardens (last stage),
1973—change of style from
quasi-Brutalist brick cliff to
more orderly, faintly vernacular

stringent government cost yardsticks, retained something of the hillside town form but without the heavy rubato of silhouette and façade. This new stage made some kind of acknowledgement to a sort of English vernacular in the form of brick ground floors with tile hanging and pitched roofs on the top stories. Here the repetitive use of long thin windows punched in to the brickwork, and the restriction to a maximum of four floors spoke of an essentially brick load-bearing construction. The long lines of exposed slab edges served the visual function of a cornice rather than indicating the concrete supporting structure behind.

The third phase of Lillington Gardens provided the basis for Darbourne and Darke's next major comprehensive housing development at Marquess Road (1970 to 1977) in the twilight area of London's Islington. Here the architects used crossover plans to give sixty per cent of the dwellings at least one room at ground floor level, with narrow windows in brick plinths and tile-hung upper stories straight from Lillington Gardens, and a tightly packed, mainly pedestrianised layout involving courtyards and meandering paths—achieving what *The Architectural Review*'s editors approvingly described as 'a reaction to the ideas of the modern monumental brigade . . . a place with a distinctive air but its own strong architectural qualities [which] fit in to their immediate surroundings and enhance the neighbourhood.' Since the surrounding houses are either ten-storeys, fifties' council houses or Victorian terraces the *Review*'s editors can only have meant that they simply approved of the style. The practice's work represented 'a significant return to that undercurrent of English environmental thinking that, because it is understated, has tended to be ignored', and which had the historical precedent of a vernacular architectural lineage

Darbourne and Darke: Marquess Road, Islington, 1977: Further development of the late Lillington Gardens style

from the Georgian model rural village through Victorian industrial model villages to Parker and Unwin's estates around the 1900s. Here was an argument akin to that of apologists of the Modern Movement, who sought to establish its roots in the respectable historical tradition of either the German classical tradition or, according to Pevsner, in late nineteenth-century English Free Architecture which, ironically, also represented the high architectural end of the *Review* writer's vernacular lineage. Style apart, Darbourne and Darke's low-rise, high density work represented a well packaged answer to sixties' conventional wisdom that high housing densities could only be achieved in high-rise building. It was not entirely surprising therefore that subsequent designers took the Lillington Gardens style on board for their own high density, low-rise designs.

Apart from a multitude of ham-fisted local authority copyists, the most notable imitation is the GLC's Odhams site in the middle of Covent Garden. Designed to a roughly similar density as the Lillington Gardens scheme (470 persons per hectare) it has the same ragged silhouette, deeply recessed windows, brick landscaping, patios and (when it grows) trailing planting—all tightly packed in a hillside village

Greater London Council architects' department: Odhams site, Covent Garden, perspective—internal courtyard, outwardly following the Darbourne and Darke style and in similar fashion concealing very complicated and ingenious close-packed plans.

Greater London Council architects' department: Houghton Regis housing, 1977—imitation of the vastly influential Palace Fields neovernacular manner

manner, though here introverted around central wells of open space. The vaguely Neovernacular forms and façades of the scheme mask the very high level of ingenuity in planning required to achieve the wide range of dwelling types and high density; for the Odhams site design achieves its apparently irregular and picturesque form in an entirely geometric and formal way, by packing, interlocking and overlapping the dwelling units together (the architects had to use models to understand what they were doing) and arranging them symmetrically on either side of a diagonal axis across the site. The inconsistencies of 'unselfconscious' exteriors in built-up Covent Garden and highly wrought plans among standard Victorian terraces do not seem to have troubled promoters of the 'simple and direct' Neovernacular style.

Sources

As an explanation of seventies' preoccupations with Neovernacular, the Rudofsky / People's Detailing / Lillington Gardens / *Architectural Review* lineage is incomplete. For seventies' Neovernacular, like NeoGeorgian (still viewed by most architects as being beyond the pale of bogusness), is no more than a revival of an earlier style in British architecture which was practised by many nineteenth-century Gothic Revival and Arts and Crafts architects, such as Butterfield and Webb, and for much the same reasons. It attempted to recall the better, more 'natural' way of life of our imagined rural heritage.

The last of the great nineteenth-century Neovernacularists was C. F. A. Voysey, whose reputation (misleadingly, that of a progenitor of the Modern Movement) has recently been revived. Voysey's primary claim to fame, apart from the inventive design of his buildings, is that he stands at the end of a more or less unbroken chain of Neovernacularism which goes back to its introduction at the beginning of century. Voysey's master in architecture was George Devey, a the distinguished designer of bogus English vernacular villages—such as Leigh in Sussex, which was designed to imitate the mediaeval antiquity of nearby Penshurst Place. Devey had spent a formative period in the studio of J. D. Harding the *en vogue* illustrator of Neovernacular cottage pattern books published in the 1820s and '30s at the height of the first Neovernacular boom.

Prompted by late eighteenth-century *chaumiers* and *Strohütten*—garden buildings and cottages in European *jardins anglaises*—the fashion for Neovernacular in Britain was started by a book by James

James Malton: Illustrations from *British Cottage Architecture*, earliest British Neovernacular text, published in London, 1798

J. D. Harding: Illustration of a
P. F. Robinson design for a
Neovernacular cottage, circa
1830

Malton, called *British Cottage Architecture*, which appeared in 1796.
Malton disliked both the 'frippery decoration' of late Rococco and the
dullness of the standard Georgian cottage: 'Its principal defects are its
uniformity, the construction of its roof, and the parapet and regular
coping around'. His rather laboured preoccupation was with the
development of a truly British cottage; 'I am most forcibly influenced
by a desire to perpetuate the peculiar beauty of the British Picturesque
rustic habitations; regarding them, with the country church, as the
most pleasing, the most suitable ornaments of art that can be
introduced to embellish rural nature'—a view which, with updated
language, few Neovernacularists would find exceptional.

Malton's designs were revolutionary for their time in rejecting both
standard sub-Palladian detailing and the brick box to which such
detailing was traditionally applied. They were essentially designed
from the inside out, the size and shape of individual rooms dictating the
final shape of the exterior. The exteriors, apart from overtly rustic
detailing in the form of rough timber posts and thatch, were given a
varied surface treatment: brick on one part, lime-washed plaster on
another, weatherboarding on another, in a way which is more than
reminiscent of the Shankland Cox Hillingdon schemes of 1978—and
which was then intended to suggest the work of an unlettered
indigenous builder's hand rather than that of a knowing architect.

Malton's book was the first of a stream of cottage books which
appeared regularly up to the 1840s, when architectural publishing
began to take the form of weekly and monthly journals. Not all the
cottage book designs were for peasants: middle-class country *cottages
ornées*, were the result of a Rousseau-influenced vogue for living the
simple life, and were larger, upmarket versions of the simpler and

cheaper peasant Neovernacular cottage. Slightly cleaned-up versions began to appear in the outer suburbs of big cities: Swiss Cottage in London for example, gets its name from a Neo-Swiss-vernacular cottage pub, built in the 1840s. But the basic peasant model was thought to be particularly appropriate for agricultural and estate workers who, under the influence of one area of fashionable thinking, were viewed for a period around 1800 as something akin to noble savages.

There are interesting if perhaps fruitless parallels to be drawn between the social backgrounds of old and new Neovernacular: an interest in primitivist doctrine, in both cases based ultimately in Rousseauesque ideas about going back to the land and simple nature; the decline of a long-reigning formalist style in architecture and a heightened public awareness of the existence of a large mass of inadequately housed people within the community.

In the early nineteenth century the act of building worker-dwellings whose rusticity of styling paraphrased the supposed noble rusticity of the occupants' lives was no more than a response to a fear of social unrest (the French Revolution was working itself out across the Channel); of a genuinely philanthropic concern about apalling rural housing conditions—and a desire to maintain a clearly differentiated class structure through the language of architectural style and form. Wealthy landlords who built comfortable Neovernacular *cottages ornées* for themselves in the country were performing something very close to the standard psychological phenonomen of identification with the potential aggressor.

It is not clear that motives have radically altered since 1800. In an attempt to give council tenants what they want—or what is appropriate for them—the Neovernacularists have been able to neatly sidestep the crucial issues of inadequate space standards and the shoddy quality of internal detailing, finishes and fittings imposed by current government housing cost yardsticks. By designing houses whose 'folksiness' and bogus village quality draw close scrutiny away from these inadequacies, the Neovernacularists are adding to this injury the insult of a patronising symbol of the tenant occupants' supposedly ingenuous, indigenous state. The vision of the village in the

William Butterfield, Baldersby St Michael, Yorks, circa 1850

C. F. A. Voysey: Design for a house near Cardiff, 1904, in a 'vernacular' style—roughcast walls, Westmoreland slate, stone window reveals and lead glazing

city is based on the premise of homes for hobbits.

Finally, it would be unfair to equate Neovernacular with Fascism—any more than it is reasonable for the Neovernacularists to equate their *bête noir*, formalism, with the same political movement. But since they do it, it is only proper to point out that both Hitler and Mussolini encouraged the Neovernacular style as a deliberate propaganda element in their programme of nationalist resurgence. Latter day instruments of the class war or promoters of the good 'old' values, or not, Neovernacularists are in bad company.

The hard edge

If Neovernacular represents the soft centre of seventies' architecture, the ostensibly tough-minded perimeter is the architecture of the hard edge, cool surface and minimal form. On the face of it hard edge designs such as Norman Foster's Sainsbury Centre at Norwich, Farrell and Grimshaw's Herman Miller factory near Bath and Piano and Rogers' Patscentre near Cambridge, to name just three recent, admired and representative hard edge buildings, are direct descendents of the Modern Movement ethic and aesthetic. Characteristics which highlight this are an absolute clarity of form, the use of the machine image, of prefabrication and standardisation, and the high value placed on sparse visual economy and the frank exposure of the elements of building. Thus, for sympathetic commentators committed to the idea of a continuously developing line of modern architecture, seventies' hard edge architecture has about it a kind of historical inevitability.

There are other ways of viewing it. In the fifties and sixties, architects tended to line up their design and themselves behind the banners of one or other of the still living Modern Movement masters, Corb or Mies van der Rohe. In those crude steps-of-the-master terms the ascendance of Brutalism represented the triumph of the post-war, pro-Corb school of tough, sculptural, plastic form and picturesque massing over the Miesians' cool, gridded, geometric aesthetic. For architects imbued with notions about progress and change in architecture Brutalism also seemed to represent a way forward out of the almost played-out formulas of the International Style. Miesian and post-war International Style buildings of this period had a distinctly dated feeling about them—pale, watered-down representations of early twentieth-century ideas and structural innovations which were no longer relevant or expressive enough for the new, dynamic non-totalitarian post-war technological age.

As other contemporary observers saw it, Brutalism was a triumph of picturesque principles of design over meaningless formalism. This argument was one in good standing in British circles where credence has traditionally been given to the notion of polarities between the romantics and the classicists, between the so-called anti-rationalists

Foster Associates: Sainsbury
Centre for the Visual Arts,
Norwich, 1978

Farrell and Grimshaw, Herman
Miller Factory, Bath, 1977

and the rationalists, between the architecture of naturalism and feeling and the architecture of order and cold intellect. In that party system the hard edge belongs to the formalist side and in the late seventies the pendulum has swung in its direction.

Whether as a result of historical inevitability or the swing of the pendulum, the loosely connected set of buildings, designs and attitudes which can be lumped together under the hard edge label has attracted many of the *avant garde* and has gained much attention from the theorists. In the same way that Brutalism developed a number of additional facets and meanings on its way from Le Corbusier to built British classics of the genre, so too hard edge architecture has acquired an intellectual and theoretical baggage which goes beyond the mere imitation of canonical Modern Movement buildings.

In the steps of the master

Apart from standard Modern Movement theoretical lore, hard edge architects could also draw on the aphorisms of Mies ('less is more', 'God is in the details' and so on), his well documented obsessive concern for detailing—and of course his buildings. Most revered of the latter was the three-dimensional composition of 'pure' planes of solid marble, glass and water of the Barcelona Pavilion, an exhibition structure of the year 1929 which existed for most people only in photographs and drawings and which thus acquired the numinous of the no-longer-earthly. Another much admired building was the

Piano and Rogers: Patscentre, Melbourn, Cambridgeshire, 1978

Mies van der Rohe: Farnsworth House, 1950

Farnsworth House of 1950, a volume of living space surrounded by glass walls and sandwiched between an elevated floor plane and the plane of the flat roof. The whole minimal assemblage was supported around the perimeter by widely spaced square steel columns welded to the edge beams of the floor and roof.

The Farnsworth House represents the practical *reductio* of orthogonal minimal architecture which Mies himself was never quite to repeat and only to paraphrase in his widely influential later fifties' design for glass-walled skyscrapers, whose simple grid pattern on elevation was merely a reference to the three-dimensional structural grid behind. Much imitated by hack post-war British commercial architects who could not be bothered to follow Mies' meticulous working out of fine-grain detail (or whose clients could not afford that kind of finesse) the true light of the master was carried through the sixties in Britain by only a small band of devoted followers, such as the Smithsons and John Winter and by the large and successful practice of Yorke Rosenberg Mardell. In Yorke Rosenberg Mardell's hand a Miesian clarity of detailing, obsessive exposure of the construction materials—usually steel—and expression of the regular structure became something of a house style, although the Calvinist ethical/aesthetic background was well understood by the practice, one of whose senior partners, F. R. S. York, had been a member of the tiny circle of pre-war British Modern Movement designers. The practice had in a sense never veered seriously from that early course, merely ringing the changes of styles as they occurred from International style through Miesianism to its present slightly uncertain preoccupation with glass skins. YRM's last major homage to the straightforward Miesian argument and the structural grid is the practice's own office building in London—a steel and glass clad steel structure, and something of a reversion after the sixties' designed St Thomas's hospital group opposite the Houses of Parliament on the south bank of the Thames, completed in the seventies. There preoccupations with a standard house style had taken over from the rigorous structural ethic and steel was masked by applied tiling—and coloured tiling at that.

Apart from YRM and commercial practices on the gridded glass wall bandwagon, there were several small pro-Miesian practices which produced variations on the Farnsworth House and earned the label of 'poor man Mieses' from Reyner Banham—an indirect reference to the fact that Mies's dictum 'less is more' had a lot to do with the high cost of getting and keeping minimal detailing 'pure'. In Britain there were few clients anyway who could afford more than attenuated versions of Mies's private houses. John Winter, probably the most distinguished of the small group of individual disciples, built his own late sixties jewel-like house at Highgate in rusting CorTen steel (which for a time was thought to be the answer to the notorious difficulty of maintaining untreated steel over the length of a building's life). However it is less an imitation of any particular Miesian building than an exemplar of Mies's

John Winter: House, Highgate
1968

principles of meticulous detailing and of the notion of expressing the inner structural framework on the exterior. Untypically for so carefully detailed a building, it was not particularly expensive.

In order to keep the room-height glass infill panels as nothing more or less than glass non-loadbearing panels, Winter introduced solid metal ventilation shutters which fit into the pattern of the steel façade grid. Embarrassingly for the purist Miesian, they are derived from Le Corbusier's proto-Brutalist Maison Jaoul.

In general terms the Miesian lessons were essentially those of architectural purity: clarity of construction methods; where possible frank exposure of the (normally steel) framework; clarity of structural design; separation of the elements of the building (for example a preference for bay-width, ceiling-height glass walls to indicate the non-structural character of infill walls) and a geometric simplicity of plan and form. From the standpoint of the late seventies it was a purity which appeared to be something akin to the classic purity of the Greek temple, which was composed of a set of standard elements—podium, colonnade and entablature—which remained constant throughout the old Greek world despite many variations in detail, planning and ornament. As the research of Jacques Paul,[32] one of Reyner Banham's students suggested, this kinship was no accident, for Mies and most of the fathers of the Modern Movement were brought up in the narrow nineteenth-century German classical tradition which laid stress on the orderliness of the classic language of architecture and which devised (or perhaps rediscovered) a series of proportional systems to which the elements of the plan and particularly the details of the façade had to adhere.

By the mid-seventies, after careful analysis by critics of the Greek temple-like National Gallery in Berlin and the leaking of Paul's unpublished research results on the architectural lecturing circuit, Mies began to be viewed as a lineal descendant of the classic tradition— not merely that of the Modern Movement but of the whole architectural tradition stretching back to the Greek roots of Western architecture. It was as if with his death in 1969 he had ascended to some kind of architectural Greek Valhalla to preside at the head of a pantheon of Modern Movement architects newly arrived at the behest of historians, in search of utter respectability for their formerly maverick heroes.

The hidden order

For a mode of architecture regularly denounced from the primitivist glades of Neovernacularism as being the product of only cold intellect, the hard edge has a remarkably mystical penumbra. At its simplest this is based on personal fundamentalist beliefs in the hidden order of nature and the cosmos—an order which at least a small group of hard edgers believe architecture should express. Fed by attitudes inherited directly from early twentieth-century scientificism, which sought to master nature by discovering the rules of its physical behaviour and its underlying geometric, mathematical organisation, this mysticism was supported by such people as D'Arcy Thompson, whose *On Growth and Form*,[33] much read in the forties and fifties and republished in the late seventies, examined the relationship between natural objects and their underlying structure and mathematical order—to take a random example, he pointed out that the mathematical Fibbonacci series was not only the basis for the reproduction rate of rabbits but also for the geometric layout of the spiral of a snail shell. It was an examination which suggested that, could they only be discovered, mathematical and geometric laws underlie even the most irregular products of nature.

In the sixties Keith Critchlow, a lecturer at the Architectural Association, had been a disciple of Buckminster Fuller and proselytizer of geodesic structures. Geodesics are based on the repetition of simple three-dimensional forms interlocking with each other, with their edges defined by the structural members. Critchlow's book[34] is concerned with representing *order* in space. The growth in understanding of spatial order seems to follow closely man's own evolution as a conscious being. First as a tool of orientation, the 'where' of things, and eventually becoming the 'how' inherent in things.

'Pattern has never been the exclusive possession of any one field of human activity; order as 'pattern' seems to have universal meaning.

The primary idea of order and number is one basis for understanding our universe.'

Subsequent articles by Critchlow and his group,[35] some of whom had formed themselves into a society known as RILKO (Research into Lost Knowledge) investigated areas increasingly outside straightforward solid geometry: the maze in the floor of Chartres Cathedral, its rose window, the Vitruvian amusium, and the mystical pattern of ley lines in the countryside and so on, all of which seemed to suggest the existence of a natural patterning and order. These inspections of the strange structural power of geodesics, the more than curious qualities of close-packed Platonic solids through Renaissance and mediaeval cosmological systems and systems of proportion and number have the quality of a latter-day Charles Fort search for the architectural philosopher's stone, which for ordinary architects seemed occasionally to veer towards the nuttily eccentric. But Critchlow was much listened to: his standard lecture (which involved the audience creating its own stable geometric structures from long cocktail sticks held together with contact adhesive) was compulsory for a time on the architecture school circuit. And hard edgers began to re-read Vitruvius and Alberti and particularly Plato, the father of purist theory and of much medieval and Renaissance cosmology and alchemy.

Of special interest to architects and designers were three of his books, *The Republic*, in which he enunciates the theory of perfect forms, the *Timaeus* in which he attempts to relate mathematics to nature, and the fragment of the *Critias* in which he describes the idealised city state of Atlantis, which will be discussed later. Essential to most of Plato's theory is the separation of the two orders of reality: 'being' and 'becoming'. The latter is represented by the world we perceive through our senses. The former, for Plato the 'real' world, is the world of intelligence—the conceptual world.

In the *Republic*, in a passage justifying the banning of artists from the perfect society, Plato makes a distinction between everyday objects of the perceptible world and their perfect 'real' form in the conceptual world. Using the example of a bed, Plato argues that what the carpenter produces is a particular bed but not the essence of bed. 'What he makes is not the ultimate reality, but something that resembles that reality.' Thus for Plato reality exists in the realm of intelligibility and not in our everyday world.

The argument has been an attractive one for theologians and particularly for architects, whose process of design involves both the notion of creating buildings which are 'ideal' for their purpose and the 'conception' of a design before it is turned into lines on the drawing board: thus the neo-Platonist Renaissance architect Alberti says: 'We can in our Thought and Imagination contrive perfect Forms of Buildings entirely separate from Matter'.

In the *Timaeus* Plato takes the Empedoclaean notion of the four constituent elements of the cosmos—earth, air, fire and water—and assigns one of the regular solids to each of them as the shape of their basic particles: the tetrahedron to fire, the cube to earth, the octahedron to air, the icosohedron to water—and seemingly as an afterthought the dodecahedron to the cosmos. In fact Plato's explanation of all this and a preliminary passage on the basic triangular geometric makeup of the regular solids is by no means clear. But the unusual properties of the regular solids which allows them and no other to nest inside each other in a precise geometric relationship; their association with the four constituents of the cosmos and their appearance in the Platonic *oeuvre* have been a stimulus to cosmologists ever since, and particularly such architectural geometers as Critchlow and other hard edge mystics who sought to discover a divinely ordained pattern behind the everyday perceptible world.

None of this re-reading of traditional Western cosmology and theory of the forms underlying nature was done at a particularly profound level. It was more a matter of a nodding-acquaintance acceptance of the Platonic notion of the existence of conceptual form beyond and behind the perceptible objects of the world, and was as much as anything an article of personal faith. What followed from that partly depended on which parts of the miscellaneous body of the great architectural arcana happened to be attractive to mysticism-prone hard edgers, or which suggested intriguing but not necessarily explicable cross-connections within the grand framework.

Water-icosahedron

Earth-cube

Air-octahedron

Fire-pyramid

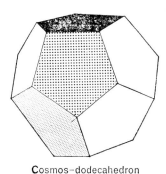
Cosmos-dodecahedron

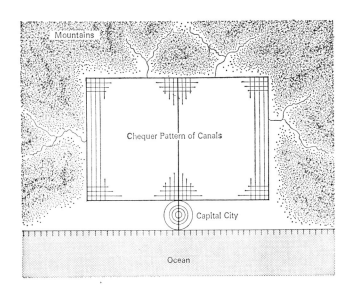

Platonic source material—the Empedoclean solids and a reconstruction of the city of Atlantis

One sideline peripheral to the details of the Platonic tradition but springing from the same attitude of mind was the interest in semiotics (discussed earlier, on page 13ff) which proposed a structure of language and meaning by means of which architecture could be classified and thus completely understood. An associated movement was the Conceptual Art of the seventies, a more-than-somewhat Platonic (and structuralist) about-face to the visual references and puns of Pop Art. Closer to the central tradition was the long-established modular co-ordination movement fronted by the Modular Society. Founded in the fifties, its ostensible purpose was to promote the idea of dimensionally standardised building materials and products in the cause of doing away with wasteful cutting on site. A necessary concomitant of this was the need to establish a set of designers' standard grid references on which standardised components could be located on working drawings. The practical usefulness of such a system has been demonstrated as dimensional co-ordination has become a partial reality. But for many adherents of modular co-ordination *per se* there lies in the background the notion of a mystical grid which approaches the Platonic notion of absolute intelligible order. The fact that the system actually works is thought to be confirmation of the existence of a greater truth and order.

More obviously related to this line of thought has been the work of architects of the central area of Milton Keynes. The whole town was originally based on a regular grid plan, apparently given subsequent bends in order to conform with late sixties' thinking which equated irregularity with 'humanism'. The Milton Keynes central area hard edgers not only straightened out the road pattern again in the area of their control but aligned the now straight roads on the midwinter sun. In one of the courtyards of the kilometre-long, rigidly orthogonal shopping centre is a hard landscape pattern which is clearly based on a

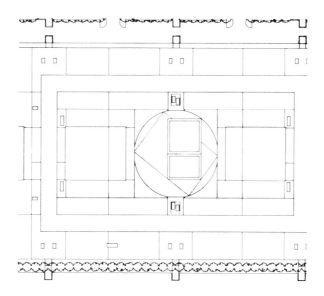

Christopher Woodward, Stuart Mosscrop et al of Milton Keynes development corporation: Shopping centre, Milton Keynes

Milton Keynes architects'
department: Design for Willen
Lake water organ

primitive astronomical symbol. Beyond the shopping complex is a large landscaped ridge which from several points of view looks remarkably like that mysterious man-made prehistoric mound Silbury Hill (a miniature replica of Silbury was proposed but not in the end built). Unobtrusive clues to this, and doubtless more hidden symbolism, are given in the names of the major avenues in the centre—Silbury and Midwinter.

Subsidiary arcana apart, some Milton Keynes architects are inclined to ascribe a kind of mystical power to the grid itself. In public pronouncements they point out that it is the traditional form of new city plans from the Greeks onwards and that, following the standard Miesian line, it provides a broad, neutral, almost notional ordering structure which does not impose particularised architectural solutions on designers who work within it. What is not said is that it is also the basic pattern for Plato's idealised city state of Atlantis, described in the *Critias* as a checkerboard of ten stadia square allotments on a naturally flat plain. It may be stretching the symbolic argument for Milton Keynes too far to point out that early designs for a circular promontory in the nearby Willen Lake bear more than a few visual affinities with Atlantis's circular coastal capital city.

The 1972 winning competition design by Jeremy Dixon and others for a new town hall in Northampton took the form of a great glass pyramid. In fact it was based on the proportions of the Great Pyramid, natural focus for a long line of speculative writing, not least the current crop of pyramidologists who ascribe natural healing powers to the form. During the design members of the team also spent a certain

Willen Lake promontory with water organ. With grid in the background over the hill, the associations with Plato's description of Atlantis may not be far-fetched.

amount of time working out the relationship of their design to local ley lines—supposed lines of 'force' which were thought to run through groups of paleolithic sites of magical significance.

These mysterious and rather private fringes of the hard edge are necessarily difficult to document fully, but in a very broad way the central belief can be summarised as an attempt to merge with and express the fundamental order and orderliness which some people believe to be intrinsic in nature. By designing buildings of great simplicity of geometry, without applied ornament, which frankly express their materials and structure, the architects of the hard edge are bringing their perceptible design close to the immutable absolute of Platonic form. There is more than a hint here of the harmony of the spheres—the perfect music generated by the mathematical relationship between the planetary orbits of mediaeval cosmology. As Superstudio, the hard line *avant garde* group in Italy once put it: 'we are interested in a still, shining form of architecture, an architecture of reason, in which the magic circle of form (as an antithesis to [disorderly] nature) may close perfectly. We are working on an architecture which we hope to render sacred and immutable'.[36]

At the more conventionally respectable academic end there was the 1940s' research of historian Rudolph Wittkower and his student Colin Rowe, now a grey eminence occasionally visiting from Cornell University in the USA. From Rowe's essay 'The mathematics of the Palladian Villa'[37] and Wittkower's *Architectural Principles in the Age of Humanism*[38] of 1949 it was clear that architects of the Renaissance used regular systems of geometric proportions of a very sophisticated kind in their design. *Architectural Principles* came out, co-incidentally or not, three years before Le Corbusier's *Le Modulor*[39] which was in many ways a re-working of the systems of proportion of the late nineteenth-century German classical tradition masters and which Corb proposed as a set of working design tools. Not much used in practice by anybody, apart from adherents of modular co-ordination, Corb's system and

Jeremy and Fenella Dixon and Edward Jones: Winning competition design for Northampton town hall, 1972— Platonic 'pure' form located carefully in the landscape in relation to ley lines.

Wittkower's revelations provided respectable confirmation of the idea of underlying conceptual form and order.

The neutral grid and the systems approach

Not many hard edgers would openly admit to having much interest in the mystical end of their mode of design. Making an aesthetic virtue of expressing and exposing the structure and doing away with ornament neatly squares with the depressed economic realities of commercial life. Orthogonal geometric form makes sense because building materials come in rectilinear shapes and in most buildings there is little point in departing from a regular geometric structural grid because it is easier to design for and cheaper to order large quantities of the same structural members and cladding materials than to have variations which must still meet the precise requirements of structural loading or function.

A British example was already to hand: the CLASP system (Consortium of Local Authorities Schools Programme), which since the early fifties had produced a large number of simple, easily and usually cheaply built schools throughout the north Midlands (see page 46). It was based on an orthogonal steel framework, more than a little Miesian in character, to which were fixed bulk-bought standard building elements—doors, windows, cladding and fittings. In the USA similar work was being done by Ezra Ehrenkrantz (who had worked with CLASP in Britain) in the form of SCSD (Schools Construction Systems Development), a structural and mechanical services system based on a regular geometry of structural members with the extensive servicing (required by a country more conscious of environmental conditioning) integrated into the roof structure and ceiling system. Its particular virtues were that it imposed very little on the shape or use of the building as finally designed by an architect. In the more or less clear floor space below the roof the designer or user could arrange and rearrange the internal partitions at will without adversely affecting the operation of the services. The designer could add whatever elevations he thought appropriate to the outside. CLASP operated in a similar fashion, although, lacking the complicated servicing package and having a tighter structural pattern, it produced slightly more stereotyped buildings.

The purpose of the systems approach was to provide a standardised way of holding up buildings and of servicing them which still allowed fine-grain designers as much freedom as possible to decide on the final 'architectural' appearance. This concentration on the ordering framework can be seen as a stepping back from perceptible, visual reality towards an ultimate conceptual order.

Flexibility and interchangeability

Parallel with this late fifties' and early sixties' interest in the systems approach was the very influential work of Cedric Price. In a series of designs for totally flexible and interchangeable structures he developed an argument for architecture as marginal, cool and neutral 'servicing', in which the built elements were devoid of values which might inhibit or direct the users or prevent them from doing precisely what they wanted. Starting with Joan Littlewood's Fun Palace of the early sixties, he produced a series of unbuilt designs which provided a minimal structural framework into which could be plugged anything from semi-permanent structures to information systems, and allowing the users to rearrange their enclosures and activities more or less at will. Price was interested in the possibilities of human activity and was inclined to jettison most of the standard architectural values as being irrelevant, applying himself to the more interesting task of providing a framework for liberation.

The only built realisation of these sixties' notions is the Interaction headquarters, in Kentish Town, London, which Price designed for this

Cedric Price: Interaction centre, Kentish Town, London, 1977

free-wheeling multi-activity community group in 1977. As with most early Price designs the primary structure is a simple framework, here a two-bay wide, two-storey high steel frame with braced two-way roof trusses. Inside this and structurally independent of it is the enclosed volume of space used by the group. Its walls are formed by vertical trusses spanning the space between roof and ground slabs and clad with standard roof decking. Inside, much of the space is at two levels, the upper floor level based on a set of square floor-height 'tables' which stand on the floor slab independent of each other and of the walls. The steel legs of the tables can be cut down to any height or extended to provide a variety of levels with relative ease. This was done during construction in the case of several rehearsal rooms. Along one side are inserted a row of two-storey site huts containing all the wet areas: lavatories, darkrooms and so on. These too are physically separate from the main structure and the 100mm or so gap between the two is bridged with a metal plate rather like the connection between railway carriages. Rooms within this main enclosed area are in most cases built from lightweight, woodwool slabs bolted on to steel angle frames, which can be extended, dismantled or recycled. Perched at one end of the primary structure is a small services enclosure and at the other end two kit-built Finnish log cabins sit on the ground, deliberately not quite lining up with the grid.

Eventually more of the primary structure will be filled in or parts taken away and the Interaction bus will park in one end as well, becoming part of the whole ensemble at various times. Price has prepared a set of instructions which should enable future users to go about the mechanical business of alterations. This is a purely technical guide and the building is designed to allow practically any *ad hoc* changes to be made.

Price's specialist use of the term 'servicing' was coincident with a new awareness of the whole issue of conventional mechanical environmental conditioning, brilliantly summarised at the end of the decade by Reyner Banham's *The Architecture of the Well Tempered Environment*, which not only set off an entirely new line of academic architectural research but provided a conspectus of gradually evolving attitudes to the aesthetics of environmental conditioning. On the one hand there were the visual possibilities of service runs in architectural composition, shown for example in Kahn's much earlier Richardson Laboratories of 1961, where the very heavy servicing requirements provided a rationale for hanging useable workspace floors between large structural towers containing the vertical service stacks and the 'service' of vertical circulation, i.e. stairs and lifts. The 1963 Queen Elizabeth Hall, designed mainly by members of the Archigram Group as part of a GLC architectural team, followed the same aesthetic rationale, although in a picturesque rather than orderly fashion: its massing and internal detailing are largely the product of decisions about the deployment of services runs.

On the other hand there was the work of Peter Foggo of Arup Associates on the three-dimensional tartan grid. This was a layout systems approach which had the same effective objective as Kahn's design for the Richardson Laboratories—that of separating working spaces entirely from servicing zones. The squares in the middle of the tartan grids were designated as work areas and the runs between the doubled grid lines as services zones. The most notable built version of this integrated servicing/planning system was the enormous John Player Horizon factory at Nottingham, details of which included the unusual Arup four-part column (which defined the intersection of the tartan grid lines on plan and provided a vertical passage for service pipes) and a man-height intermediate floor level used entirely for

Arup Associates: Horizon factory, Nottingham, 1968

109

Opposite
Horizon factory—interior drama
of service piping

services. At the Horizon factory the exigencies of production processes meant that parts of the three-dimensional grid had to be left out to accommodate machinery and services (the grid or rather lattice became notional in these spaces, which for any neo-Platonist was perfectly reasonable) leaving the thick spaghetti-work of extract ducts in shining metal exposed in a number of cases outside the servicing zones. This *mélange* of ductwork bears, however coincidentally, a close visual resemblance to the Brutalist sculpture of Edouardo Paolozzi and has evidently remained evocative for subsequent hard-edge designers. Clad as it is in vaguely Brutalist materials, the Horizon factory can hardly be said to belong to the hard edge aesthetic. But external appearance apart, it does gesture firmly in the direction of a neutral ordering framework which allows users maximum flexibility—here not the denizens of Price's Fun Palaces or his nationalised linear universities, the Potteries thinkbelts, but engineers reorganising plant processes.

The internal drama of otherwise boring services ducting at the Horizon factory cannot have been entirely unintentional for it bore more than a little relationship to designs by the Archigram Group, many of whose visionary schemes of the sixties had been composed from blown up more or less recognisable air conditioning components. There were also affinities with student preoccupations with the visual possibilities of extending colour coding (used by production engineers as a simple identification system or for piping) into a 'functional' decorative coda to the basic pattern of a building.

Notes on 'as found'

This interest in the high art possibilities of everyday objects stands firmly within the British 'as found' tradition, whose roots are probably ultimately in Dadaist ready-made art (for example Duchamp's 1917 *Fountain*: a 'found' unretouched urinal on its back with the artist's pseudonym painted on the base) and in sixties' Pop art, notably in the work of Richard Hamilton whose *Toaster* and *The Critics Laugh*, the one

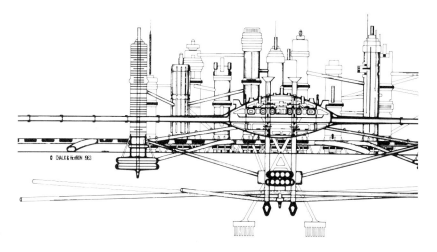

Ron Herron and Warren Chalk: Interchange project, 1963. Typical of early sixties' Archigram imagery of high architectural technology which has been vastly influential on the high flyers of the hard edge.

Charles Eames: Case Study
House, Pacific Palisades, Los
Angeles, 1949

a standard high-style Braun toaster with Hamilton's name in place of
the Braun logo and the other a Braun electric toothbrush with a set of
dentures in place of the brush, were particularly memorable for
architects because the basic found elements were modern classics of
product design rather than anonymous raw materials.

Fine art apart, the canonical example of found architecture was a pre-
Hamilton design, the Eames Case Study House of 1949. The American
designer Charles Eames had reversed the normal design process of
creating a house design and then choosing the materials by starting off
with American builders' suppliers catalogues and assembling his
design, rather like a kit of parts, from readily available components:
glazing, wall cladding, fittings and so on. Much admired as a paradigm
of the architecture of mechanisation and essentially Miesian in
appearance, the approach to design was deliberately anti-hand-crafted.
Protagonists of the mystical grid would argue that here was yet another
way in which the conceptual grid or lattice could flexibly accommodate
a variety of design approaches.

In England, the Smithsons' Hunstanton School of 1954 emulated this
found approach to design. All the materials comprising this co-
incidentally first British Miesian building were left more or less as they
had arrived on site and were simply assembled together: precast
concrete floors, a steel frame of standard rolled steel joists welded

Team 4: Reliance Controls,
Swindon, 1968

together and (after a coat of protective paint) left exposed, washbasins simply bolted to a horizontal steel member and drained via plastic pipes into an open floor level drain below, and so on.

Inherent in this attempt to make architecture a direct response to life rather than an example of hand-crafting (in the sense that life, in the form of the real building world, was then and is now about scarcity of materials, diminished standards of craftsmanship and standardisation in the material and components industry) was a restatement and updating of the vernacular argument. In the way that primitive men went about building by using whatever materials and tools happened to be to hand, so too modern architects, divesting themselves of the past (which in the Smithsons' time still meant the 'corrupt' style of the Victorians), used whatever happened to be available locally in their own society. In practice this meant using things like steel joists, standard windows and doors, servicing equipment, and products readily available on the market. For Pop fine artists, whose basic argument was devised in the late fifties in the Independent Group (to which the Smithsons belonged) building materials were replaced by the new found elements of contemporary society—the images of popular picture journalism, advertising, motor cars, household objects and photographs—often collaged together in unexpected ways to create ironic, funny and ambiguous comments on both popular culture (which the Pop artists enjoyed but about which they were not entirely serious) and the new art itself.

The serviced shed

From the systems approach of people such as Ezra Ehrenkrantz, the total flexibility approach of Price and others, bits of Eames and Smithson found aesthetic in conjunction with the discovery of the visual possibilities of servicing technology, and against the background of Pop art's redeployment of boring and ordinary elements in new memorable visual contexts, there developed a hard edge architectural type which Reyner Banham aptly described as the 'serviced shed'. Not entirely surprisingly it has been developed primarily through industrial building.

The Reliance Controls Factory, designed by Team 4 (Norman and Wendy Foster and Richard Rogers) in 1967, was reckoned at the time to be a turning point in built factory design and represents the modest beginning of the serviced shed aesthetic. Apart from its slightly Miesian exterior of profiled plastic-coated steel decking attached to a framework of rolled steel sections and braced by diagonal tension ties, it provided a network of services in the floor and a secondary network of ventilation and lighting in the roof, leaving large areas of clear floor space for the assembly of electronic components. In subsequent designs Foster repeated the same servicing formula, succeeding jobs increasing their emphasis on ceiling routes and on even less expressive elevations than the Reliance factory—a neutrality which is to be found in most of Foster Associates' subsequent work.

In their passenger terminal for Fred Olsen Lines at Millwall Dock the long barrel vault leading passengers to their ships is a monoque construction based on two skins of plastic-coated corrugated steel with the minimal services running along a trough suspended from the top of the vault. The amenity centre built for the same company nearby is a two-storey construction with services in the roof and first floor, faced

Foster Associates: Fred Olsen Lines Passenger terminal, walkway

Foster Associates: Modern Art Glass headquarters, Thamesmead, 1973

with reflecting glass. The Modern Art Glass offices and warehouses at Thamesmead uses a standard minimal portal frame building of the style readily available off the peg from manufacturers of industrial buildings but given an all-glass gable end wall employing new technology fixings and neoprene gasketting in place of traditional transoms and mullions.

In 1971 Foster's old partner, Richard Rogers, joined with the Italian architect Renzo Piano who had designed several notable systems approach buildings in the late sixties in Italy. These had combined inventive new lightweight structures and cladding composed of individual elements repeated over and over: grp roof pyramids acting dynamically with lightweight steel tension members, lightweight prefabricated cladding over simple braced metal framing, and exposed services in both roof and perforated floor beams.

Already in 1970 Richard and Sue Rogers had designed a model for a standard house to be made from zip-up, snug seam, heavily insulated, aluminium sandwich panels with gasketted windows wrapping over the eaves line and with a totally flexible interior. Since more panels could be zipped on to either end, it was capable of infinite extension. In the Piano and Rogers UPO Fragrances factory at Tadworth (1975) the architects applied the same aesthetic, though here modified by the larger spans which demanded trusses rather than a self-supporting roof and a new technology sandwich panel in insulated glass reinforced concrete. Inside this big shed are arranged the various activities of the factory: administration, laboratories, manufacturing and warehousing, each zone differentiated internally by acoustic partitions, flooring and ceiling treatment: suspended ceiling in the offices and laboratory, durable plastic floors and exposed trusses with exposed and colour-coded services running through. But as Andrew Rabenek, British high priest of the systems approach (and an associate of Ezra Ehrenkrantz) pointed out, the components making up the building were all purpose made: 'when architects try to push forward building technology beyond the bounds of ordinariness, there is invariably a price to pay.

Piano and Rogers: UPO
Fragrances factory, 1975

Richard and Sue Rogers: Zip-up
house design, 1970

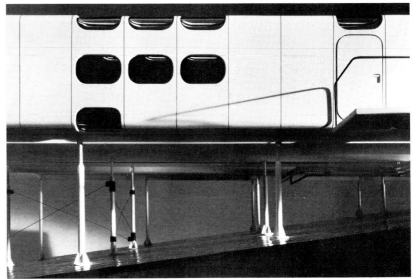

Because the hardware in current production does not quite match the
style or image they are seeking for the building, then they are obliged to
meet the demands of the image by craft means, often with less than
immaculate results'.[40]

At their 1974 Habitat warehouse and showrooms at Wallingford,
Ahrends Burton and Koralek made a 'found' virtue of the less than
immaculate fixing detailing of standard corrugated asbestos sheeting.
In this pair of structures with rounded eaves lines, bullnose corners
and, inside, a dramatic tubular steel spaceframe roof, the crude
standard fixings for the corrugated sheeting merge in with the
complications of exposed services ducts running through the frame.
Each element is distinguished from the other by bright colours. Like the

Piano and Rogers scent factory the exterior is painted a bright colour, there bright yellow, here deep green.

At the same time both the aesthetic and argument of the heavily serviced shed was being worked out at Milton Keynes in the form of a series of standardised advanced factory units. Milton Keynes had, at the beginning of the seventies, an urgent need for new factory space. Starting with a fairly standard pitched-roof structure the corporation very quickly erected several thousand square metres of factories at Walter Eaton, deploying a very deep fascia panel to hide the pitched roofs and to create a sense of orderliness in keeping with the grid layout. Together with a parallel development at Mount Farm, the Milton Keynes' architects began to work on a more ideal neutral system which was given flesh in a prototype erected in the grounds of the

Ahrends Burton & Koralek: Habitat warehouse, Wallingford, 1974

Milton Keynes architects: advanced factory units, Kiln Farm, 1975

corporation headquarters at Wavendon. A square Miesian building, with an exposed frame nine bays wide and three bays high, it allows for a mezzanine floor inside and for great flexibility in the exterior elevations. In fact the building has proved its flexibility, for not only has it changed colour twice (as well as having its interior completely changed to suit the information organisation which replaced the architects' department) but the cladding panels and windows have been changed over a period of time as well.

Roughly the same structural system was used for advanced factory units at Kiln Farm, but with a completely different cladding system. Composed of small bright yellow $1 \times 2m$ pressed metal panels, it owes more to motor car engineering technology than to the building industry. Windows are gasketted, panels can be used horizontally or vertically and door and window panels are interchangeable with the standard blank panel.

In several buildings of late 1979, at Warrington New Town and Gillingham, Kent, Farrell and Grimshaw developed the total flexibility idea in sleek-surfaced factory buildings which combined readily available components (such as roller shutter doors) with industrial cladding and purpose made all stainless steel toilet units in buildings which were cheap, rapidly erected, heavily insulated and immensely stylish.

Farrell and Grimshaw: Factory at Warrington, 1979

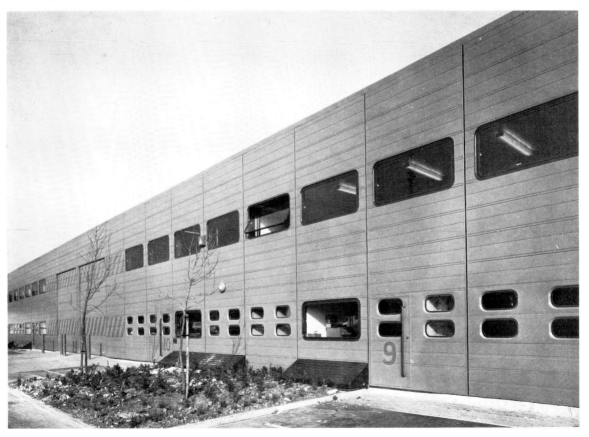

Almost all of these big serviced sheds rely on bright colours, profiled panels or exposed structural grids for their external aesthetic. Foster Associates' tendency to use a single surface, preferably with only a thin eaves detail or even (apparently) none at all, is best exemplified by its design for SAPA's aluminium extrusion works at Tibshelf near Derby. Unusually for buildings which are designed to be extendable and totally flexible, the original 1973 building was actually extended four years later in exactly the same style and, to begin with, without any apparent joins. The exterior is composed entirely of white demountable panels fixed to a simple steel frame and with openings on one side for delivery trucks. Fosters would probably have preferred a big coloured box-like shed but the local arch-conservative planning authorities recommended white to them, although even then there was a planning appeal over this non-colour. With as bland an exterior as it is possible to design, the interior is, like most serviced sheds, very highly wrought and colourful: vast Paolozzi-like extract ducts and brightly colour-coded surfaces and pipe runs, with most of the servicing in the trussed roof or on the roof itself: the 'found' aesthetic becoming a little too knowing to be entirely that any more.

Most of these big serviced sheds wear the factory aesthetic easily

Foster Associates: Sainsbury
Centre for the Visual Arts,
Norwich, 1978

because they are factories. But the same approach has become acceptable for other types of buildings as well. Fosters, for example, designed the Sainsbury Centre for the Visual Arts at Norwich in 1978— a vast hangar clad in panels of profiled aluminium hung on a truss structure (walls and roof are in the form of trusses). Inside, the services, lavatories and kitchens are ranged within the outer wall zone and the

Michael Hopkins: House,
Hampstead, London, 1977

various functions of the centre are simply located in slices cut across the plan. The entire inner surface of the building, apart from the floor, is clad in white metal louvres which allow selected, silhouetted views of air extract equipment—suggesting that Foster had played out and here cooled down the somewhat overheated use of the found aesthetic.

The concept of a factory or neutral enclosure was applicable to domestic buildings as well. Michael Hopkins, formerly with Fosters, built a house for his family in Hampstead in 1977. Planned on two floors with a circular staircase near the centre of the house, only the bathrooms and a store are enclosed by fixed partitions. Elsewhere, the family's activities are defined by venetian blinds which also provide the privacy needed with front and back walls entirely of glass. Flanked by side walls in profiled heavily insulated steel decking (which also forms the two ceilings) the structure is a simple steel frame with exposed lattice beams, supported internally on steel columns on a 2×4m grid. A minimal house in several senses (it was cheap, composed of small structural members and very thin framing details, and constructed from a very limited range of materials: glass and steel) it owes not a little to the Eames Case Study House in both form and the use of light (rather than the traditionally Miesian heavy) members. The open plan happens to suit Hopkins' family at the moment but the design allows for a wide range of subsequent alterations and divisions as their needs change.

The cool surface
There are local precedents for Hopkins' use of glass but they echo old Modern Movement preoccupations with glass as a building material and as a symbol: there was the pure visual excitement of nineteenth-century examples from Decimus Burton's Palmhouse at Kew and Paxton's Crystal Palace onwards; there were late nineteenth-century *avant garde* educational theories which made connections between growing plants under glass and growing young minds. And glass represented the man-made form of pure immutable crystalline structure. Mies said in the twenties 'We can see the new structure principles most clearly when we use glass in place of the outer walls . . . The use of glass imposes new solutions . . .'.[41]

While in practice Mies uses glass as the transparent infill for his structural bays, several of his designs for skyscrapers of around 1919 show the exteriors enclosed in what appears to be a continuous skin of glass. Evocative images for post-war British architects, because they appeared in most of the standard texts on the Modern Movement, they were nevertheless difficult to conceive of in reality because of the need to frame glass panes of necessarily limited manufactured sizes set in transomes and mullions. With the introduction of tinted reflective and mirror glass around the beginning of the seventies it became possible to approximate the original skin-like ideal by using framing, painted or anodised to the approximate tone of the glass, or by using aluminium frames which tend to have almost the same reflective quality as mirror glass.

Foster Associates' exploration of this theme at the IBM building at Havant and the facilities centre at Olsen Lines' Millwall Dock were attempts at the all-glass skin. In both cases the framing, and significantly the thickness of the eaves were reduced to mere lines. York Rosenberg Mardell had followed the same theme in their office building at the Hague, where they used a pattern of square panes all over the cubic mass of this free-standing building and in their own offices in 1977, where they used a more complicated pattern. Christopher Dean's Leicester University Library presents a reflecting glass front wall to an open square, next door to the faceted glass skylights of Stirling and Gowan's engineering laboratories. Dean's building follows the ideal of a glass enclosure with heavy servicing and exposed structure inside in an unusual fashion. Here service runs and ducts are built into hollow structural columns and beams: a heavy concrete version of the integrated services structure approach done elsewhere in lightweight metal.

By the late seventies the all-reflecting glass building had begun to achieve cliché status as neoprene gasketting technology and the use of structural glass cantilever ribs reduced the need for heavy framing and allowed the use of unframed corners—as for example in Michael Manser Associates' offices for Howard Humphreys and Sons at Leatherhead. But although the form of free-standing buildings suggested a nod in the direction of pure crystalline form there remains more than a suggestion that it was really a fashionable updating of the outworn aesthetic of the fifties' curtain wall.

In pursuit of the minimal crystalline enclosure, Foster Associates developed the design for the extraordinary Willis Faber Dumas headquarters at Ipswich. Here the site was not the open industrial landscape setting of many of their earlier buildings but an irregular plot

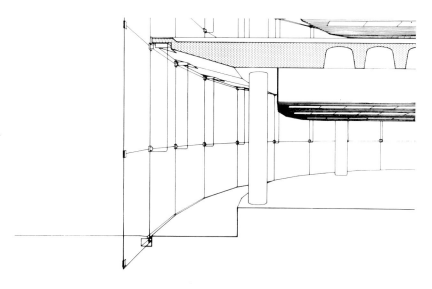

Foster Associates: Willis Faber Dumas headquarters, Ipswich, Suffolk, 1975. Section showing all glass wall (left) hung from thinned edge of floor slab and stiffened by vertical glass fin.

123

bounded on one side by a small open space, on another by an urban motorway lined with fifties' and sixties' office buildings and on the other side by the edge of the old winding town centre street network. Unexpectedly from an office noted for its strict adherence to orthogonal geometry, the dark glass wall of the building simply follows this meandering perimeter. Apart from small metal plates at the junction of the glass panels and the occasional metal door cantilevered up out of the floor slab, the three-storeyed façade is entirely of glass. The faceted, irregular form immediately recalls a shining obsidian extrusion which has been forced out of the earth, cut off square at the top and then solidified—and in so doing has contracted slightly, forming a narrow 200mm deep gap between pavement edge and the glass surface.

Apart from its crystalline associations the building is in a sense a standard heavily serviced shed, a neutral enclosure with an apparently free-standing structure inside. This free-standing effect is emphasised by the visual uncertainty of the glass walls' structure and by the yellow painted perforated ring beams which run around each of the three visible slabs set nearly two metres in from the wall line. The floors of concrete waffle slabs are supported by circular columns painted bright yellow. The upper two floors contain office accommodation with a small area on the turfed roof (originally intended to be a helicopter pad) given over to cooling towers and executive offices. On the ground floor one side contains the plant for the services, the other computer areas and in between, behind the escalators and facing the entrance, is a

Foster Associates: Willis Faber Dumas headquarters, Ipswich, Suffolk, 1975

125

swimming pool. None of this is immediately obvious from outside because of the different degrees of reflection and transparency in each of the glass panels, which give the passer-by occasional glimpses of shining mechanical plant, brightly coloured yellow and green slab edges, columns and flooring, interspersed with reflections of the buildings opposite. Simple heavily serviced shed with the mechanics exposed inside or not, its complex and fundamentally ambiguous external form takes it beyond the realm of the serviced shed aesthetic.

Variations

Serviced sheds tend to have relatively simple structures: steel columns, trussed roofs and, apart from Arup's large span bays at the Horizon factory, a structural grid of relatively small scale. But slightly before Ehrenkrantz's SCSD shed prototype, Konrad Wachsman had been experimenting in the USA with spaceframe structures. Unlike trussed roofs, spaceframes are three-dimensional lattices of small lightweight members based (like the geodesic dome) on the repetition of such geometric patterns as the tetrahedron, which themselves are fundamentally stable. Unlike trussed roofs the supports for spaceframes need not be around the perimeter and may be point supports. That distinction was for a time important for some architectural moralists who objected to two-way truss roofs since they looked like spaceframes but structurally were not.

At the 1974 Wellingborough Medical Centre designed by Aldington and Craig (formerly designers of cool neovernacular sixties' housing) the space-frame is actually made up of tubular steel V trusses at right angles to each other, forming a grid of square bays on the top and bottom chords. Although the size of the members is, in spaceframe fashion, consistent throughout, the whole roof structure is in fact a truss composite resting partly on blockwork internal walls. Inside, the air conditioning pipes which serve both open areas and enclosed consulting rooms (which have their own roofs under, and quite independent of, the main roof) swoop and snake in an apparently disorderly but sculptural way through the lattice above. Outside, the edges of the roof are canted back in an imitation of the triangular geometry of the edges of spaceframes, here in fact following the profile of the V lattice trusses. Underneath, the blockwork walls of rooms project beyond the eaves line itself, having a stepped-back plan somewhat in opposition to the ethic of the neutral cover which the interior seems to suggest.

A similar roof is to be found at Ahrends Burton and Koralek's Maidenhead Library of 1973. Here the square roof, in space frame fashion, is supported entirely on eight columns located near the four corners, two to each side of a corner. The loads from the roof are transmitted to the top of the columns by inverted open pyramids in tubular steel. The envelope is glass. At high levels it is canted following the diagonal line of the inner members of the roof frame, a line which is carried down the sharply chamfered brick 'buttresses' which read as incidental attachments to an all-glass two-storey high wall. The failure of the inside structure, in critics' eyes, to live up to the drama of the exterior has probably something to do with the absence of now fashionable roof-hung services runs (apart from light fittings) and the simple non-space frame engineering design. Maidenhead nevertheless represents the direction of less flexible building versions of the big shed, here demonstrating how, using isolated spaceframe-like supports, the external skin need not read as four vertical planes and can operate as a further element separate from the supporting structure and the roof.

Rather closer to the spaceframe is the roof to the Goard Burton Partnership's office in Yorkshire. It is based on a series of tetrahedra which produce deep, chamfered-off eaves (as, but for slightly different reasons, at the Maidenhead library) and is clad entirely in glass. For reasons more of simplicity than anything else the whole frame is

Ahrends Burton & Koralek: Maidenhead library, 1973

Goad Burton Partnership: House, South Milford, Yorks, 1974. Designed as the partnership office it was envisaged that it could be turned into a dwelling. After severe obstruction from the local planning committee an appeal to the Department of the Environment was successful.

supported on columns around the perimeter. It is a little flexible serviced shed in the sense that its function and layout are changeable. It has in fact been converted from an office into a house by reorganising the enclosed bathrooms and erecting small enclosures for bedrooms. Not for nothing did the *Architects' Journal* bill it as a 'controversial crystal': an immutable framework containing the vagaries of humanity within.

It is typical of the fundamental conservatism of British patrons that the most highly wrought of the big sheds should be by British designers but carried out for a Parisian client, the French government. Designed by Piano and Rogers and the engineer Ted Happold and the winning entry in an international competition, the Pompidou Centre is a big shed inside out: six large clear floors enclosed by a glass skin but with all the structures and services runs and most of the circulation *outside*. In fact much less flexible than something like Price's Interaction Centre, where the floors as well as the vertical partitions are changeable (although Happold originally envisaged moveable floors), the Pompidou Centre deploys both sensational structure, brightly coloured vertical air conditioning stacks and *ad hoc* walkways in a gesture towards flexibility. Services and walkways appear not with proper British rectitude merely inside the upper zone of the ceiling, but out

Piano and Rogers: Centre
Nationale d'Art et de Culture
Georges Pompidou, Paris,
1977—the major built
realisation of Archigram's early
sixties' imagery

front and over the top, forming on the two long sides of the glass-
skinned shed both vertical, diagonal, horizontal and zig-zagging
tubular elements in primary colours and transparent glass, serving the
conventional rôle of elevations. The neutral enclosure is observable
only from inside, where around the perimeter and beneath the long

trusses and coloured services runs it acts as a blank background to library, museum, industrial design centre, acoustic research centre— or whatever the managers of the structure decide they need.

In additon, the Pompidou Centre is the realisation of British designs of the sixties by (apart from Cedric Price) the Archigram Group, whose concern was to design not merely flexible, almost dynamic machines (and in the case of Ron Herron's Walking City actually dynamic machines) in and among which a great variety of activities could take place, but structures whose component forms were related to the image of integrated servicing and highly advanced and loaded-up structure. The serviced shed ethic and aesthetic results not only from the work of those old Modern Movement designers but from the heroes of *avant garde* sixties' design as well.

It can be argued that the big serviced shed is the inheritor of the Modern Movement mantle. For, unlike supposedly Modern Movement buildings whose reinforced concrete structure is covered up by brick-rendered walls, the big shed's structure—steel cladding and trusses, grc and grp panels with nuts and bolts and ductwork—is plainly on view and is a clear expression of industrial culture. If the big shed is on occasion capable of greater expressiveness, as for example at Maidenhead, nevertheless the solid geometry of the basic form is the realisation of the Modern Movement urge towards anonymity, towards a mode of design which does not rely on external ornamentation or picturesque form for its visual impact but rather on a clear, serene and neutral form. Where Mies could only dream about glass skins and reflections and faceted transparent structures, in the seventies new jointing and structural glass technology and inventive architects have brought the dream to life.

The neutrality of the serviced shed is by no means negative, for the lack of articulation in plan, the separation of the skin and roof structure from the interior structure and the addition of servicing has enabled these buildings to be more or less genuinely flexible and intechange-able in their functions. Whether or not those things are necessary or desirable in most buildings, the serviced shed has developed an aesthetic of its own, an aesthetic which is itself capable of great flexibility: from the almost totally neutral and inexpressive white shed of Foster's SAPA to the highly articulated *ad hocness* of Price's Interaction Centre.

New cookbooks

The deployment of found structural and high technology elements in hard-edge architecture and of found imitation rustic materials and shapes in Neovernacular are two different expressions of an otherwise standard predeliction for returning to purer and simpler architectural forms. The found theme also forms an important background to the low and high art versions of seventies' preoccupations; which have come to be respectively known as *bricolage* and *cuisine minceur*. The latter (critic Peter Murray's transmogrification from French cooking terminology) is a reference to French chef Michel Guérard's new way of cooking which retains all the classic principles of French cuisine but abandons the high-fat and high-carbohydrate ingredients traditionally used and replaces them with subtle new combinations of otherwise familiar ingredients. It is a label which very neatly describes the high-style opposite of the architectural farmhouse cooking of *bricolage*.

Bricolage

For a period in the mid-seventies, the term *bricolage* had a special, although not entirely justified, significance for architectural structuralists and semioticians. In Claude Levi-Strauss's canonical *The Savage Mind*[41] the French anthropological theorist makes an introductory note about the distinction between the engineer and the *bricoleur*. To repeat a then much quoted passage 'the bricoleur is still someone who works with his hands and uses devious means . . . adept at performing a large number of diverse tasks but unlike the engineer, he does not subordinate each of them to the availability of raw materials and tools conceived and procured for the purpose of the project . . . his rules of the game are always to make do with whatever is at hand . . . the engineer is always trying to make his way out of and go beyond the constraints imposed by a particular state of civilisation while the bricoleur by inclination or necessity always remains within them'.

This passage has been much quoted, among other places in Jencks and Silver's *Adhocism* of 1973.[42] This was a collection of Pop and popular found 'bricolaged' images which Reyner Banham was to dismiss knowingly as representing the discovery by the authors rather

Charles Moore: Talbot House, 1964

late in the day of what any real life mechanic found himself doing in the workshop when putting a lash-up together. Banham was also to point out that the Levi-Strauss passage was not part of an anthropological argument but an incidental preliminary passage: 'Much as the parable of the Good Samaritan appears in the gospel less to claim virtue for Samaritans than to make a point about the nature of good neighbourliness, so the *bricoleur* is there less to claim virtue for do-it-yourself than to illustrate a point about the nature of mythologies—that they are cobbled up *ad hoc* out of folk tales and fables that are to hand, rather than purpose designed to explain the Cosmos'.[43] Mis-transliteration from a fashionable text or not, the word *bricolage* has passed into architectural parlance and its more commonplace original sense of *ad hoc*, cobbled together and *gauche* makes it a useful term for the low-art end of the development of the found theme in seventies' British architecture.

US sources

American examples of this approach were to hand in the late sixties. Apart from alternative building assemblages such as the flattened car bodies of Drop City, there was Charles Moore's Talbot house of 1964. Here Moore provided a basic design for the external shape and disposition of rooms and left the builder to effectively get on with the detail design—by putting in whatever stock doors, windows and skirtings, etc, he happened to have in his yard. Subsequent designs by

Moore and his circle deliberately employed elements such as 'supergraphics' (giant-sized stripes and patterns devised by a graphic artist more familiar with the scale of the printed page); deliberately cheap finishes such as rendered plasterboard and plywood; deliberately gawky construction involving cheaply painted building timber and corrugated plastic; carefully chosen old-fashioned fittings found in builders' supplies catalogues (a reference to the Eames Case Study House); and neon signs, in one case in a dining room for respectable and conservative academics at Santa Barbara.

Partly inspired by Pop art, this was a reaction to the conventional architectural aesthete's objection, well represented by Peter Blake's denunciation of uncontrolled US building development *God's Own Junkyard*,[44] to makeshift commercial hoardings and signs, sprawl and unco-ordinated clutter which was characteristic of the American main street. But for the new aesthetic it represented a contemporary *bricolage* of human elements which, when viewed altogether had a vernacular exuberance and liveliness of its own. It was a *bricolage* affectionately summarised in the writings of Tom Wolfe and in the Venturis' *Learning from Las Vegas*.[45] In this celebration of the primitive commercialisation of the Las Vegas strip the Venturis pointed out 'architects who can accept the lessons of primitive vernacular architecture . . . do not easily acknowledge the validity of the commercial vernacular', which in their view represents 'real' American culture and is thus an appropriate quarry for contemporary architectural sources.

The British response

The discovery and new approval of American *ad hoc bricolage* could not have a real equivalent in Britain. Here exuberant brashness was not part of the cultural scene and in any case the 1947 Town and Country Planning Act was specifically designed to prevent it from occurring in cool, tasteful post-war Britain. Nevertheless by the mid-seventies careful research, prompted by this new obsession, had revealed the existence of some indigenous examples from before the operation of the act. These tended to be on the seaside along the south coast or in East Anglia. One such development was named California, presumably in homage to tract layouts and more certainly to the home of the popular culture of the thirties. Blackpool, whose permanent fairground buildings and illuminations represented a potential parallel to the neon façades of Las Vegas, had become simply a living monument to the post-war days of modest excess, its imagery institutionalised and fixed. There have even been proposals to list the central area as one of protected buildings.

Best of the British *bricoleurs'* work was Jaywick Sands in Essex. Discovered by Tim Street-Porter, the brilliant architectural photographer and chronicler of Pop culture, Jaywick Sands was a 1930s seaside development near Clacton-on-Sea consisting of weekend

chalets on miniature 125m² plots, without drainage or water. The mostly two-room houses were nearly all self-built from standard door and window units, using interlocking asbestos tiles and the local and cheap traditional materials—weatherboarding or pebbledash—all painted in garish colours and decorated with verandas and porches. Roads are named after popular and later Pop American motor cars—Daimler and Buick Avenues among them. For Pop-oriented architects this was not shanty town jerry building but an indigenous British paradigm of the way twentieth-century *bricoleurs* respond directly to their exigent circumstances. Appropriately enough, though, Jaywick Sands is now under threat from the local authority which wants to erect a new housing development; this will inevitably be in the Essex Neovernacular of cosy closes and informal 'indigenous' groupings.

Jaywick Sands has served less as a visual model for imitation than as justification for seventies' designers in Britain who opt for a knowing *bricolage* (rather than Neovernacular) style. The element of knowing means, in Pop style, not taking the original model with utter seriousness. There is always a jokey element, a covert two fingers to both establishment and popular taste which is disguised with innocent protestations about designing for ordinary people or designing in an 'ordinary' way. Naturally enough architects will never admit this in public and very few British clients have sufficient self confidence to allow their buildings to represent anything other than progressiveness, propriety or apparent affluence. When buildings have a financial life of sixty years, as they do in Britain, it is difficult to find an opportunity for irony—the joke wears a little thin. Unlike in America, building in Britain is generally funded directly or indirectly by central government or large institutions, and the element of artfulness is about all British architects are given to play with. It turns out to be an artfulness in getting around the received wisdom of the design guides and DOE inspectors; in making do with familiar, cheap materials but in an unexpected way and in using whatever high or low technological innovations happen to be around at the time, all hung together with intelligence and easy good humour. 'There ought to be more pursuit of making the familiar strange—to distort it, invert it or transpose the everyday ways of looking and responding which render the world a secure and familiar place' argued Basildon New Town *bricoleur* Clive Plumb in a discussion of public housing in 1974.[45]

Plumb's own work both as a public and private architect represents the *bricolage* way out of the Neovernacular impasse. His Langdon Hills estate at Basildon New Town is at first sight organised in the Italian hillside manner, with red mono-pitched tile roofs sweeping down a low hillside. But the layout—fingers of terrace houses attached to one side of a cranked spine—is based not on a broken-up Radburn layout but on computer studies of maximising land use carried out at Cambridge by Lionel March, and on an understanding of minimising heat losses and overshadowing via the profile of the typical house section, its orientation and the fall of the land. These, together with a walk-through service duct for all the piped services (including television), which doubles as a retaining wall on the treacherous clay foundation soil, are highly sophisticated in technical terms but are worn lightly in the total design.

The rows of houses are stepped down the site and separated by access roads, parking spaces, pedestrian walkways and steeply sloping back and front yards. Inside typical houses all the services and the bathroom, kitchen and storage room are on the ground floor, with a double-height dining/playroom opening on to two bedrooms. Above, under the high end of the sloping roof, is a long narrow bedroom next to an open living room. These rooms are lit by windows in the external wall and a skylight in the roof which also lights the dining room below and the kitchen. This is a common enough internal arrangement in architect-designed private houses but is entirely uncommon in public housing.

Outside, the two-storey back wall is clad in prefabricated timber

Clive Plumb: Basildon development corporation, Langdon Hills, Essex, 1974

Clive Plumb: House at Ross-on-Wye, Herefordshire, 1972

panels with applied strips and on the other side the architects have used concrete blockwork for the house walls and brick for the hard landscaping and retaining walls. With red concrete tiles and the band of patent roofing sheet into which the skylights are set, there is a sort of mixture of materials which Neovernacularists are inclined to recommend. But with the exception of the brickwork, almost all the materials are peculiar to the seventies, none of them are local and their combination is decidedly quirky. Blockwork, normally only used as an internal walling material plastered over, was finally agreed to by the Basildon housing committee because of a nationwide shortage of bricks and, it should be said, after Plumb's team had persuaded manufacturers to produce blocks of a reasonable colour and quality and found a team who were good at laying them. Only on the spine row and at the junctions with the 'fingers' does the gritty, deliberate visual awkwardness develop into a cosier quasi-Neovernacular mode.

Not much publicised by the corporation is the fact that most of the internal walls are non-structural and can safely be removed by enterprising tenant *bricoleurs* who may wish to rearrange the somewhat unconventional internal layout into something more to their taste. The obvious cheapness of the interior materials acts as an encouragement.

Langdon Hills' awkward section was first developed on a small house at Ross-on-Wye which Plumb designed in 1972. Here the plan fans out from one corner with the living room, orientated towards the sun, wrapping around at ground floor level and enclosed by two flank walls which express the line of the roofs and the unexpected angle of the skylights, which quirkily form a transparent collar around the neck of the focal mass.

Plumb's next house for a client in Essex demonstrates his preoccupation with diagonals and the division of geometric masses by transparent strips—shown in practice by a strip window which wraps over a complicated geometry of roof planes from the entrance hall on one side to the living room on the other. Where the Ross house had (if

the deliberate gawkiness of the gable ends is ignored) a clear geometry, the forms of the Essex house turn out to look almost entirely *ad hoc*. The materials—pebbledash, timber with applied strips, brick and glass— are all put together with an improvised panache. The owner was the builder and, when materials were not available and his building knowledge faltered, he relied on his architect to act as a sort of foreman and materials-finder. In the hinterland of that part of Essex there exists a network of people and backyard industries which is a happy hunting ground for the twentieth-century *bricoleur* in search of *ad hoc* things to make his building work.

In a more recent house, this time for himself in a village near Chelmsford, Plumb was finally caught by the *Essex Design Guide* net. At Langdon Hills, Essex Council had been unable to intervene because its sphere of planning control did not extend to the new town development area. At Great Leighs where it does, there was nothing else for Plumb to do but design a 'vernacular' external skin and out of sight an all-glass internal courtyard orientated towards the sun with new low-technology solar water-heating panels. Built almost entirely by himself and friends the house is too well detailed and built and too cool in its geometry and selection of materials for it to make much more than an ironic comment on how to do comfortable architect's architecture within the Neovernacular straightjacket.

The best-documented case of knowing *ad hoc bricolage* is Ralph Erskine's housing development at Byker in Newcastle-on-Tyne. Clearly megastructural in its intentions, it consists of a tightly packed agglomeration of low-rise housing over a sloping hill, encircled and protected from the prevailing wind, the new tube line and a proposed urban motorway by a cliff-like wall up to seven stories high and two rooms deep, which snakes around the northern perimeter. On the windward side the wall presents a brick face punctuated by small

Ralph Erskine: Exterior of Byker wall, Newcastle-on-Tyne, 1975

Ralph Erskine: Interior of Byker wall

soundproofed windows and embellished with brightly coloured, sound-dampened ventilator boxes. The bricks, in five basic colours, are laid in vast patterns over the wall which intensify in complexity around the few openings for motor cars and pedestrians—halfway between high-art mural and arbitrary bricklayer's use of whatever brick stack happened to be nearby. This and the adjacent corrugated plastic and rough timber car ports and the bright blue prisms occasionally visible on the roof give only an intimation of the *bricolage* content of the interior of the development.

The inner side of the 'wall' is clad miscellaneously in concrete asbestos sheeting and brick. Hung on this face are a series of rough timber balconies and walkways and high level crossovers (to a series of 'rib' blocks which step down the hill to merge into the low-rise housing), all in bright primary colours with occasional shed-like roofs in corrugated plastic, and planter boxes and seats. The low-rise housing incorporates a large number of existing public facility buildings such as schools and health centres (the wall itself contains the old Byker bath house which now supplies hot water to the flats adjacent). Arranged in a series of short terraces and small squares, the housing is hung with rough timber pergolas and downpipes, fences and dustbin stores (with concrete planting boxes sitting on top) and roofed in profiled steel surfaced with brightly coloured plastic. The absence of a clear geometry in the layout (whether grid or Radburn) adds to the impression of jumbled makeshift.

Bricolage is not always easy to get right, as Erskine's own contemporary housing scheme at Eaglestone in Milton Keynes demonstrates (see page 75). There, in a private development for middle-class buyers, the carefully calculated disorder of Byker is replaced by folksy detailing in the form of bow windows, rough timber work and cosy closes; the nicely judged half bricolage, half stylish design of Byker's brickwork appears here in the form of arbitrary changes in the colour of bricks and concrete roofing tiles.

Byker's brightly coloured roofs and bricolage elements are also to be found in Edward Cullinan's Highgrove housing estate for the London borough of Hillingdon. Otherwise quite unrelated to Byker, it accepts the 'found' element of the suburban road and strings four rows of double sided housing along two streets whose scale is dictated by pre-1977 rules of highway engineering and a contemporary government directive banning garages in public housing.

The scheme is a *bricolage* searcher's goldmine: constructivist multi-functioning details in the form of arrangements of plastic overflow pipes protruding from gable ends; the location of grilles and deflector plates of balanced flues to boilers as part of the pattern of the façade; industrial roofing in bright blue brought down at the gable ends to form two ears edged by over-large plastic gutters which shoot water into rainwater butts (which are the effective main roof downpipe and are made from civil engineering-scale concrete piping). The bright blue industrial roofing system was used because it is self-supporting and is therefore economical to construct. All these and the somewhat farmyard quality of the house section (which like Byker and Langdon Hills allows for modestly dramatic interior spaces), and the omission just before the contract started of garages and boundary walls, contribute to the *ad hoc* quality of the place. It allows tenants to sprawl comfortably and untidily across their back lawns without, as in a regular orthogonal housing layout or a carefully cosy Radburn scheme, spoiling the orderliness of the architect's original lines.

Cuisine minceur

Cullinan's *bricolage* is partly related to his own personal experience of building houses and having to inventively redeploy materials and components intended for other uses. But there is also in his work an element of high-art bricolage or *cuisine minceur*: a deliberate redeployment of high architectural motifs and techniques in what, at

Edward Cullinan: Highgrove
housing, Hillingdon, 1977

Highgrove, is otherwise supposed to be a low art, low-rise housing estate. At the top of the site, both blocking the view up two of the paths which are part of the primary pedestrian network and also acting as a focal point, is a pair of semi-detached houses. In both cases the entrances, the focus of attention, are splayed back and undercut and given sets of consequential, 'architectural' half columns, rather in the manner of eighteenth-century sham temples at the ends of the *allées*. These two paired houses are also highly diagramatic in the sense that despite their consequential appearance they are merely the standard house section sliced in half with the raw edges chamfered off. In a sense this is making do with the forms to hand rather than devising forms for the occasion. For architectural gourmets, the end walls of each terrace in pale yellow ochre rendering are not a little reminiscent of both Palladian farmhouse prototypes and Palladio's Mannerist device of

superimposing temple fronts (which the designers hint they would
actually liked to have painted on the end walls)—here reduced to a
primitive silhouette.

An earlier design of Cullinan's for refurbishing the interior of a turn
of the century country house for Olivetti (for which James Stirling
designed the new teaching wings) followed the same approach, here in
both style and method. Cullinan relocated the main entrance in the old
service courtyard, simply facing the old walls with a new skin of brick
(which allows a service void between old and new) and erecting a
lightweight open framing for stairs and cross circulation above in white
painted steel tubing, with bent piping handrails and thirties' standard
lamps—all reminiscent of early twentieth-century seaside and

steamship design. The same details are to be found on external fire escapes and ramps and, in a slightly different manner, in semi-tetrahedral dormer windows to study bedrooms, light fittings throughout the house and prism-shaped and circular internal windows. Here *bricolage* has almost turned into a deliberate stylistic eclecticism which looks back to suburban everyday design rather than to the more customary high architectural sources.

Some architects have been whole-heartedly prepared to rein-vestigate the possibilities of high architectural eclecticism. Martin

Martin Johnson: House for
Graham Ovenden, 1978

Johnson's house for the painter Graham Ovenden at Liskeard is representative of a very small field. Designed as a studio and as a setting for Ovenden's collection of period furniture it is being built gradually with the help of only one workman. Johnson's design incorporates elements from high Victorian gothic, Spanish villa and seaside self-build together with Art Nouveauesque details of both Johnson's and Ovenden's invention. Built in solid granite with marble flooring it will eventually have spires and turrets and ground-level flying buttresses, a stone-vaulted hall and decorative cast iron work on the ridges. Though it may be an appropriate setting for a member of the group of 'Ruralist' artists newly dedicated to the old, to ordinariness and to a slightly upmarket Victorian primitivism, for mainstream architects the house reads as little more than an updating of the Italian miniature town designed by Clough William Ellis at Portmerion, Wales.

Architecture *cuisine minceur* had by the second half of the seventies become the special preserve of the young practice Campbell, Zogolovitch, Wilkinson, Gough, designers in the late sixties of some of the most inventive London boutiques. (Knitwit in South Moulton Street, for example, made an up-to-date reference to the newly canonised painter David Hockney rather than the then fashionable psychedelia of the King's Road.) Like most young practices, they have completed more designs than buildings, but the few completed schemes indicate how radically the practice has moved from the aesthetic and ethic of both the Modern Movement and its seventies' inheritance.

Avowedly in search of architectural images which people can enjoy (rather than the immutable architectural truths of architecture), the practice loads up and mixes its architecture rather than stripping back to the bare essentials. In the process they use whatever forms and style happen to be available and appropriate. In their Bridport riverside cafe they designed a building which on first inspection looks exactly like a riverside cafe: a set of three lightweight timber pavilions with big windows attached to the front of a standard two-storey house. Closer inspection by even the most rudimentarily trained historical eye reveals a series of details from the last seventy years of architect-and-builder design: Wrightesque overhangs on the dormers, Jaywick Sands two-storey timber additions at the back, the continuation of the gables to form flank walls penetrating into the two end pavilions (designed originally to be terminated by big concrete balls from suburban brick fence design), Odeon doorways with the bracing bar slanting in the wrong direction, unexpected oriels and triangular-headed windows upside down.

At Phillips West 2, the restyling of the exterior of an auctioneer's showroom and the addition of office space and maisonettes, the practice added bulging balcony railings across the front, a Wrightesque roofed lift tower and a courtyard at first-floor level surrounded by a Roman tiled veranda on thin timber posts. Behind, the entrances to the maisonettes (whose brick stairways swoop up in a series of S shapes) mask the ocean-liner open tread stairways. The colours are pale pink and white and grey and navy blue—a palette which elsewhere has included pale greens and blues and is hardly calculated to meet the approval of architects whose current preference is still for muted tones of brown and dark green or alternatively primary colours, especially green. For them, Campbell Zogolovitch Wilkinson Gough have revived not only the forms of interwar untutored popular taste but its garish colour preferences as well. Countering that point of view is the fact that

Campbell Zogolovitch Wilkinson Gough: Phillips West 2, Salem Street exterior, 1977

the practice's sophisticated clients do not particularly conform to the
discreet norm and seem to like their buildings.

The practice claims not to have an immoveable affection for the
interwar suburban model, but to pick the style for each job as it comes.
This is born out by a recent design for a housing development in
Chelsea where the overall form is rather like a squared-off three-
dimensional spiral which descends from a high block of flats at one
corner with two adjacent façades in carpenters' Modern Movement
with false pediments and big windows and then two following façades
which turn into a sculptural, vaguely updated Gaudiesque mode
complete with pinnacles.

In another design for a shopping/entertainment mall the practice has
combined existing façades in Georgian, Regency, Victorian and early
twentieth-century commercial styles with their own versions of
Seaside Regency, Picture Palace, eighteenth-century Oriental and other
less clearly identifiable styles in a brilliantly coloured display which is
as far removed from the puritan hard edge Modern Movement aesthetic
as it is possible to go.

Architecture *cuisine minceur*, in the sense that styles from the recent
past are what are to hand (especially after the popularising of the
Moderne and Art Deco) and perhaps less the *bricolage* of deploying
available materials in unexpected ways, Campbell Zogolovitch
Wilkinson Gough's work suggests that an exploration of the uses of
stylistic eclecticism by inventive designers may well form one of the
ways beyond the end of the Modern Movement.

The view from here

The view from the end of the decade is of a British architecture which is alive and well in parts. But given the financial and bureaucratic exigencies of a declining economy it is not surprising that for some commentators there is a certain *fin de siècle* quality about the whole proceedings. Far from connoting a richness of inventiveness and design, British architecture's modest variety of styles and attitudes and its growing interest in the apparently unserious—an interest in impermanence, flexibility, in the joke, irony and the frivolity of knowing eclecticism and stylism all represent a state of affairs paralleled by the irresponsible 1890s or even the decline and fall chronicled in Gibbon's great work. The architectural calvinists tend to take the cataclysmic view.

There is, it needs to be said, something going for the cataclysmic or at least profoundly unhopeful view even for optimistic followers of architecture. For the British setting for the practice of architecture is inimical. The profession is in search of new ground rules. There is dogged mediocrity in housing design and an unacceptably low level of technical competence and costing know-how in its execution. The official planning bureaucracy is deeply conservative and anti-architectural. There exists a widespread self-delusion about the supposed virtues of the British architectural past and a desire to preserve it at all costs. The body of major patrons, most of them the huge financial institutions, display an unusual determinedness to be safe and dull. It is a case of the unenterprising inflexibility in pursuit of the indifferent.

Yet the architecture chronicled in earlier chapters has come about in those difficult circumstances and in many cases despite them. What has not been chronicled is the inordinate number of delays and the number of times each scheme has had to be redesigned at the behest of planners determined to perpetuate extant mediocrity in the name of 'fitting in' and of officials who police a set of building regulations of undoubted worth whose extraordinary length and Kafkaesque legalese has rendered them seriously unintelligible and lacking in credibility.

Yet architecture of considerable quality has come about in the decade in Britain. What is missing is a sufficient amount of it and, more significantly, the exuberance of form, colour and imagination to be found in contemporary architecture across the Channel and the Atlantic. Even at its small-scale end, British Neovernacular looks tame and neo-council-house when viewed against European work of a similar sort—especially that of the French designers of the Mediter-

Richard Rogers Associates: Design for Lloyds Bank, City of London, 1979—an unusual case of establishment client bravery

François Spoerry: Port Grimaud, France. Momentarily a completely convincing recreation of a Mediterranean seaside village

Jean Baladur (controlling architect): Apartment block, La Grande Motte, France, 1977

ranean coastal resorts, whether at the stunningly accurate pastiche of Port Grimaud or the quasi-Corb, quasi-vernacular of the Languedoc littoral, which make unconsciously ludicrous but enthusiastic sets of cross references to the vernacular of the Mediterranean which inspired the post-war Corb and provided Bernard Rudofsky with rich photographic pickings among architecture without architects.

Nor is there anything to be found in Britain to parallel the vast, fantastic and blindingly coloured summer apartment buildings sanctioned by controlling architect Jean Baladur at La Grande Motte, or Emile Aillaud's *trompe l'oeil* apartment towers at Nantes or the fantastic geometries of Piet Blom in Helmond, Holland—to name but a few relatively commonplace European designs.

Nor is it likely that Rogers Associates' Lloyds Bank design for the City of London will repeat either the structural and servicing bravura of their Pompidou Centre or its brilliant colouring. Or that either that practice's or Norman Foster's design for large-scale developers in the last years of the seventies will be more than discreet reminders of their earlier then-sensational work outside the metropolis.

The standard architectural and lay view from Britain is that all this is just as well, so firmly ingrained are habits of decent and colourless mediocrity. It is almost certainly this national inclination to think grey and to accept the oppressive burden of Ruritanian bureaucratic control, rather than any lack of architectural imagination, which has turned the greater part of British architecture into an interesting local study, but internationally probably something of a *cul-de-sac*. That at least is the view of Philip Johnson, former senior acolyte of Mesianism and now George Burns-style impressionist and tailor-in-chief for the

148

new architectural clothes of the emperors of US big business. In a visit in 1979 to Britain he lavished praise on architects of the hard edge school as inheritors of the Modern Movement mantle. At the same time he pointed out that for him and for *avant garde* designers in the USA the Modern Movement was an irrelevance.

In his own work and in the designs and buildings of such US architects, loosely known as the Post Modernists, as Robert Venturi, Charles Moore, Stanley Tigerman, Cesar Pelli and Richard Meier he had demonstrated a knowing contempt for the rigid orthogonalities and austerity of calvinist Modern Movement design in favour of large scale, eclectic frivolity, to use an apt but calvinist term. None of these architects works in a recognisably similar style, some garner their sources from the architecture of the past, others make knowing references to Modern Movement design itself, others draw their sources from the 'bad taste' commercial vernacular of the USA. Many of them do all these things at the same time or in succeeding building commissions.

This effusion of individualism in the USA goes against the traditional view that architecture should represent a continuous line of evolutionary development, as these designers well know, and there is something of the cheerful defiance of the early stages of Pop painting of the accepted mores of architecture which take on a special significance because of that.

What has been built in recent years in the USA is viewed with a kind of wistful but horrified fascination by British architects—for in the dawning Post-Energy days it seems that the serious future must be guided by the grey rules and mores of economic recession and of the irresistable urge to seek solace in reflections from the past—an architectural past which at the beginning of the decade was viewed as largely banal and grubby, aptly expressive of a long grim chapter in our social history.

If British built architecture no longer leads the world in giving both visual and occasionally cerebral pleasure to its beholders, Britain still remains, curiously, a major focus for the world *avant garde*. The international architectural mafia continues to pay close attention to arguments conducted in a small circle of London architectural schools and in the pages of the British architectural journals; it visits London regularly and watches alertly for new studio drawing board design from young designers and students in the British orbit.

That may be good for British architectural *amour propre*, and if the considerable body of young talent is not decimated by the seductions of teaching or building abroad it may auger well for the eighties. But it augers little for the immediate visual future peopled by banality-bent patrons, earnest but crazed bureaucrats devoted to the letter of incomprehensible regulations and prohibitions—and a public audience starved for too long of the real pleasures of the best of contemporary British architectural design.

Notes

[1] Martin Pawley, 'Into the void of Post Modernism', *Building Design*, 23 September 1977

[2] Nikolaus Pevsner, *Pioneers of the Modern Movement*, London, 1936; re-issued as *Pioneers of Modern Design*, 3rd rev. ed. Penguin, Harmondsworth, 1975

[3] Siegfried Giedeon, *Space Time and Architecture*, Harvard University Press, Cambridge, Mass, third edition, 1956, page 6; Oxford University Press, London, 1967

[4] David Gebhard, 'The Moderne in the US 1920–1941', *Architectural Association Quarterly*, July 1970, page 5

[5] Reyner Banham, *Theory and Design in the First Machine Age*, Architectural Press, London, 1960

[6] Notably the group surrounding Tim Benton and his A305 television course on twentieth-century design

[7] David Watkin, *Morality in Architecture*, Clarendon Press, Oxford, 1977

[8] See for example Reyner Banham's review of David Watkin's book in 'Pevsner's Progress', *The Times Literary Supplement*, 17 February 1978

[9] Piers Gough, 'Belle epoque is just around the corner', *The Architect's Journal*, 21 and 28 December 1977, page 1217

[10] Martin Pawley, 'Into the Void of Post Modernism', *Building Design*, 23 September 1977, page 12

[11] Charles Jencks, *The Language of Post Modern Architecture*, Academy Editions, London, 1977

[12] Charles Jencks and George Baird (editors), *Meaning in Architecture*, The Cressent Press, Barrie & Rockliff, London 1969

[13] Christopher Alexander, *Notes on the Synthesis of Form*, Harvard University Press, Cambridge, Mass., 1964

[14] See for example Geoffrey Broadbent, 'A plain man's guide to the theory of signs in architecture', *Architectural Design*, vol 47, 1977, pp 7–8, and David Dunster, 'Sign language', *Architectural Design*, November 1976, pp 667–669

[15] Robert Venturi, *Complexity and Contradiction in Architecture*, Museum of Modern Art, New York, 1966; Architectural Press, London, 1977

[16] Cedric Price, Frank Newby and Robert H. Suan, *Air Structure, a survey commissioned by the MOPBW*, HMSO, London, 1971

[17] Graham Stevens has made two films: *Atmosphields*, 1971 and *Desert Cloud*, 1975

[18] Reyner Banham, *The New Brutalism*, Architectural Press, London, 1966

[19] Banham, *ibid*, page 127

[20] Ivor de Wofle, *Civilia*, Architectural Press, London, 1971 and *The Architectural Review*, October 1973

[21] *Building Design*, 5 January 1979

[22] Patrick Nutgens, 'Towards the future', in Barbara Goldstein (editor), *Architecture: Opportunities, Achievements*, RIBA Publications, London, 1977, page 97

[23] Christopher Alexander, *Notes on the Synthesis of Form*, Harvard University Press, Cambridge, Mass., 1964

[24] Bernard Rudofsky, *Architecture without Architects*, Museum of Modern Art, New York, 1965

[25] *Whole Earth Catalog*, various editions

[26] Nicholas Taylor, *The Village in the City*, Temple Smith, London, 1973

[27] Oscar Newman, *Defensible Space: People and Design in the Violent City*, Macmillan, New York, 1972; Architectural Press, London, 1973

[28] Conrad Jamieson in, for example, 'Modern Architecture as an Ideology', *Architectural Association Quarterly*, vol 7, no. 4, pp 15–21

[29] John Nobel, Keith Elvin and Ron Whitaker, *Residential Roads and Footpaths—layout considerations*, report published by the Department of the Environment and the Department of Transport, 1977

[30] Oliver Cox, ' ''People's Detailing'' at Hillingdon', *Architectural Review*, October 1978

[31] *Architects' Journal*, 1 November 1978, page 816

[32] Jacques Paul, 'Modern Architecture and the German Classical Tradition', unpublished thesis, University of London, 1973

[33] D'Arcy Thompson, *On Growth and Form*, Cambridge University Press, Cambridge, 1942

[34] Keith Critchlow, *Order in Space, a design source book*, Thames & Hudson, London, 1969

[35] Keith Critchlow, *Into the Hidden Environment*, Philip, London, 1972 and *Chartres Maze, a model of the universe*, 1976; John James, 'Mediaeval Geometry', *Architectural Association Quarterly*, vol 5, no. 2, 1973; Tine Kurent, 'Stonehenge and the Vitruvian Amusium, *Architectural Association Quarterly*, vol 7, no. 3, 1975

[36] Quoted in Jim Burns, Anthropods: new design futures, London, 1972

[37] Colin Rowe, 'The Mathematics of the ideal villa and other essays', MIT Press, London, 1976

[38] Rudolph Wittkower, *Architectural Principles in the Age of Humanism*, (Warburg Institute Studies, vol 19), London, 1949; 3rd rev. ed. Tiranti, London, 1962

[39] Le Corbusier, *Le Modulor*, English trans. Faber & Faber, London 1954

[40] Andrew Rabenek, 'Factory, Tadworth, Surrey', *Architectural Review*, December 1974

[41] Claude Levi-Strauss, *The Savage Mind*, Weidenfeld & Nicolson, London, 1966

[42] Charles Jencks and Nathan Silver, *Adhocism*, Secker and Warburg, London, 1972

[43] Reyner Banham, 'Bricologues à la Lanterne', *New Society*, 1 July, 1976, page 25

[44] Peter Blake, *God's Own Junkyard: the planned deterioration of America's Landscape*, Holt, Rinehart & Winston, New York, 1964

[45] Robert Venturi, *Learning from Las Vegas*, MIT Press, London, 1972

[46] Clive Plumb in a talk to the Chelmsford Chapter of Architects, 11 December 1974

Index

154